T0267062

ADVENTURE AWAITS

KRISTIN LENZ

HARVEST HOUSE PUBLISHERS
EUGENE, OREGON

Published in association with William K. Jensen Literary Agency

Cover design by Bryce Williamson
Cover photo © franckreporter / Getty Images. Back cover images © mammuth, borchee / Getty Images
Interior design by Nicole Dougherty
Interior illustrations © Ana Iacob, struvictory, Moto-rama / Getty Images
Photos on page 51 and 87 by Stephanie Jolin Photography
Photos on pages 187, 219, and 224 by Autumn Richards
All other photography by Kristin Lenz

For bulk, special sales, or ministry purchases, please call 1-800-547-8979. Email: CustomerService@hhpbooks.com

ADVENTURE AWAITS

Copyright © 2024 by Kristin Lenz
Published by Harvest House Publishers
Eugene, Oregon 97408
www.harvesthousepublishers.com

ISBN 978-0-7369-8882-7 (hardcover)
ISBN 978-0-7369-8883-4 (eBook)

Library of Congress Control Number: 2024931388

Printed in China

24 25 26 27 28 29 30 31 32 / RDS / 10 9 8 7 6 5 4 3 2 1

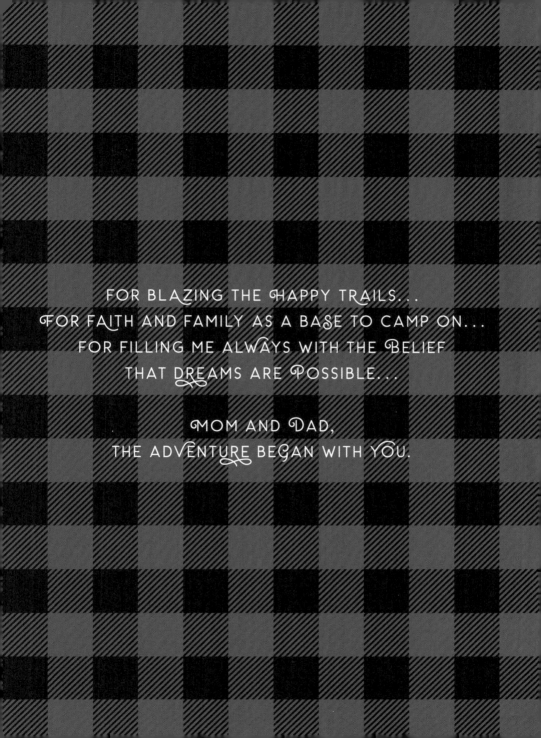

FOR BLAZING THE HAPPY TRAILS...
FOR FAITH AND FAMILY AS A BASE TO CAMP ON...
FOR FILLING ME ALWAYS WITH THE BELIEF
THAT DREAMS ARE POSSIBLE...

MOM AND DAD,
THE ADVENTURE BEGAN WITH YOU.

CONTENTS

FROM MY NECK
OF THE WOODS

Throughout my day, I have conversations with women of many different ages, in different stages and walks of life. These conversations happen within my circle of friends, among my coworkers, and with the ladies in my Bible study and in my book club. They happen with fellow moms, with customers who come into my shop, or with my followers online. There are common themes that emerge, even in small talk:

- Does what I'm doing matter?
- Life has changed a lot recently; what will I do now?
- Do I have the courage to try?
- Do I have what it takes to make what I'm doing great?
- Can I gather the gumption to go in a new direction?
- Am I enough?

Have you been asking these questions too?

I've had all the same thoughts. They've entered my heart and mind often in life changes over the years: graduating from college and starting my first job, getting married, starting a family, changing careers, creating my own business, looking toward empty nesting. Life has been a journey—one that has brought a lot of lessons along the way.

My life journey began as a young girl in the bluebonnet fields of Texas. I moved north to Iowa for college and my teaching career, then headed further north, finding a haven in the Northwoods of Wisconsin. In each location, I've grown and learned through the events, situations, and relationships I've experienced. My faith has grown the most.

I can look back on each route I took and see that God has been mapping the whole adventure. At times, I took some wrong turns—went left when I should have gone right. There were some dirt roads, some bumpy ones, and some with spectacular views.

The drives through the hills and valleys are what have given me strength. Even though I'm always looking for more mountain tops, the valleys have been where I've found the resources: the wellspring of wisdom that instilled my resilience to continue my forward trek.

So join me; let's journey together through these pages. We'll be road-trip buddies as we explore what God has planned next for our lives.

Constantly using our map (God's Word), we can travel closer and closer to True North (God) and the flourishing life He has planned for us.

Maybe it starts with a dream you have in your heart.

When I was in high school, I took my first trip overseas, to France and Switzerland with my French club. The item I was most excited to pack was my new travel journal. I wanted to remember the details of the whole experience. That's how I suggest starting this journey too.

Plan a little outing to a favorite bookstore or shop, and pick out a special journal to record and hold your thoughts as you go. Then pick a spot—whether at the bookstore, a coffee shop, a park bench, or a corner café table—where you can open up that journal and write your name and the date inside. Now write a letter to yourself, commemorating this first day of journaling so you can look back on it later and see how far you've come. As you get into the chapters,

I'll provide you with Journal the Journey questions, prompts, and lists to help you connect with your ideas.

Inside each chapter, you will find some fun extras and activities to help you blaze your trail with encouragement and focus. You'll also make connections as I share some of the special blessings of Northwoods living and ways you can add them into your life no matter where you live.

This book came about as people started hearing my story and the leap of faith our family took moving to a lakeside log cabin in the woods ten years ago.

For several years before our move, my husband and I had been hearing our friends Bill and Colleen share about times "up north" at a cottage with their family. Over dinner one night, I asked why they loved it so much. Their response was instant, and it changed our lives: "The two best things you can do for your family? Teach them to love God, and buy a lake house." We took their wisdom to heart, already working on the first one and searching out the second.

In moving to the Northwoods, I found a unique and special place—for not only its beautiful location but also its traditions and way of life. Many of these have become metaphors in this book, as this time in nature—surrounded by the beauty of God's creation, of woods and water—has ministered to my soul and sprouted journeys worth the adventure.

My message in these pages isn't to go out and buy a lake house but to be awakened to the possibilities out there waiting. God is pointing the way. He's traveling in front of you, behind you, and right by your side.

I'm so excited to share more of my story with you and give encouragement for yours.

LET'S GO NORTH!

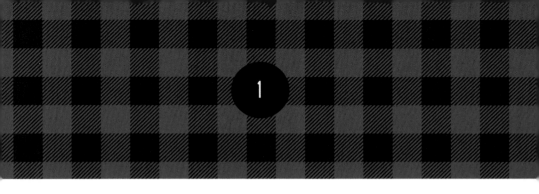

FOLLOW THE ARROWS

"For I know the plans I have for you," declares the LORD,
"plans to prosper you and not to harm you, plans
to give you hope and a future."

JEREMIAH 29:11

Throughout the Northwoods, white arrow signs point toward restaurants, churches, stores, camps, cabins, cottages, and homes. These arrows, crafted from wood and painted white, hang one on top of the other from trees or posts at intersections and road turns. They point right or left, letting you know in which direction your destination lies. The iconic symbol inspired the name of my company and blog, White Arrows Home.

I've come to see how those same white arrows can be reminders of the Lord's leading in my life. I see and recognize directions from God as the arrows always pointing the way.

When we first moved to the Northwoods, I was looking for where I was supposed to go and what I was supposed to do with my time. The youngest of my five children was starting kindergarten. After being a stay-at-home mom and community volunteer for the past 13 years, what was next for me? I looked at my past. I listened to my heart and what I loved spending time doing. And I reflected on those things that I had always thought "What if?" about, like starting a blog where I could take my love of decorating and use it to write, share, and inspire others.

What an adventure I've had since writing that first blog post. I've opened a brick-and-mortar shop with an online store, co-launched a podcast, and written this book. I've also made amazing friendships and connections along the way that have enriched my life.

God is directing you, too, based on your own unique gifts and talents, to flourish in your life.

A FLOURISHING LIFE

A life lived to the fullest—one that is flourishing and fulfilling—will look different for all of us. But there are a few things that will show up in each scenario. How can a life that flourishes be defined? It's one where we are always growing and developing in a healthy way. It means placing ourselves, when we have the choice to do so, in a favorable environment with encouraging people around us. Flourishing is being willing to go through the work—it's the adventure of moving forward to improve and make progress in all ways: spiritually, personally, and professionally.

In a life that thrives this way, we know our bodies are special, and we treat them as such by getting enough sleep, eating well, hydrating, and staying fit and active.

Living a flourishing life doesn't mean we won't have trials, struggles, and sadness. What it does mean is that we know that even through those moments when times get hard, God will use the adversity for good. We can grow and be stronger because of them.

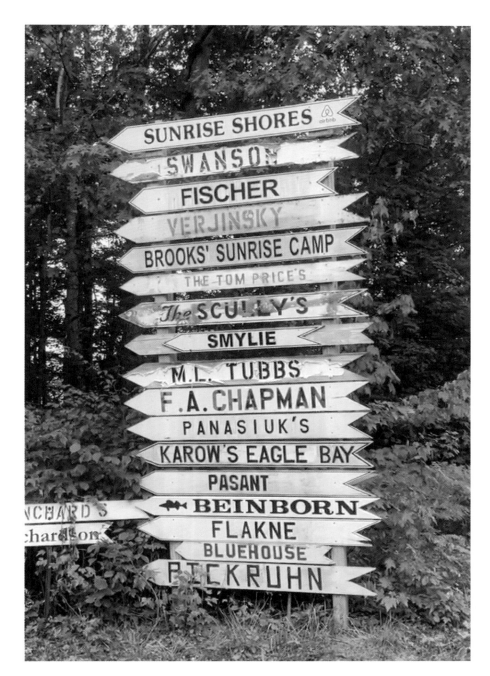

> I SEE AND RECOGNIZE DIRECTIONS FROM GOD AS THE ARROWS ALWAYS POINTING THE WAY.

WHO WE ARE

Before we can take a risk, before we can move forward toward a dream and a flourishing life with confidence, we need an understanding of who we are. We must be honest about how we see ourselves, how we've been influenced (either favorably or badly) by others, and most importantly, how God sees us.

Our personality and character play a part in how we view ourselves and how others view us. And that's just the beginning. Think about how our families, our birth order, and our decisions—good or bad—all come into the mix. But none of these things have the final say in who we are and who we are becoming. Only God has that authority.

In the book of Exodus, we meet a special Hebrew baby boy born in Egypt during a time when the Hebrews were enslaved by the Egyptians. Pharaoh was afraid of their growing numbers and ordered that all Hebrew baby boys be killed at birth, thrown into the Nile.

So when this child was born, his mother hid him for three months. When she could hide him no longer, she followed the directions of Pharaoh—but with a twist. She did put her baby in the Nile River, but safely inside a woven basket. She left his fate to God.

As he floated, the waters brought him by Pharaoh's daughter, who was bathing in the river. She decided to raise the baby as her own and named him Moses, which means "draw out."

I love how that's exactly what God wants to do with us today. He wants to draw us out and into His glory with lives that are evidence of His power. He wants to draw us out of our depression, out of our laziness, out of our selfishness, out of our present struggles—whatever they may be. There are abilities and strengths within us that are meant to shine. God wants to pick you up out of the uncertain waters and place you on your path of purpose so you can use your gifts to serve, lead, and thrive.

GUESS WHO

If you're questioning whether you do have gifts and if God has arrows in place for you to notice, follow, and be encouraged by, then let me share something with you. Maybe we've never met, but I know some things about you. I do.

Have you ever played the game Guess Who? One person thinks of a well-known celebrity or historical figure while everyone else asks questions to figure out who the person is. See if you can guess who I'm describing with the following verses (just a few of the many verses that could be referenced to describe this person):

chosen by God (Ephesians 1:4)

loved (1 Thessalonians 1:4)

God's workmanship created to produce good works (Ephesians 2:10)

friend (John 15:15)

citizen of heaven (Philippians 3:20)

light out of darkness (Ephesians 5:8)

righteous and holy (Ephesians 4:24)

redeemed and forgiven (Romans 3:24)

Guess who? It's you.

This understanding of who we are is part of the foundation that, when set firmly, will hold us up. Along with this understanding, we want a footing

that does not shift, have an expiration date, or go out of style. That solid-as-a-rock base is Jesus. He—and who we are in Him—forms the foundation that never changes.

GOD WANTS TO PICK YOU UP OUT OF THE UNCERTAIN WATERS AND PLACE YOU ON YOUR PATH OF PURPOSE SO YOU CAN USE YOUR GIFTS TO SERVE, LEAD, AND THRIVE.

TAKE IN THE VIEW

When we're sure of who we are and have secured our foundation, we can pause to survey the view. Let's take inventory of the places, actions, and ideas that beckon. Let's identify our passions.

Some of my passions have long been decorating my home and entertaining. Another thing I care deeply about is encouraging others. God gave me the gifts of hospitality and encouragement. I also believe He gave me gifts for writing and teaching. These gifts and passions birthed many of my recent dreams.

About ten years ago, I started a journal, and on one page, I listed these passions along with a few others: faith, family, friends, fitness, food, fun. When I revisit that list, it gives me such joy and reminds me of God's faithfulness. Those passions have remained the focus of what I put my time into and what shapes and fills my good life.

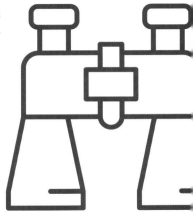

The journal you've started for this journey will be one of the ways you will be able to take in the view of all God has done and is doing in your heart and life. Take time right now, with pen in hand, and journal through a few things.

»⊦→ JOURNAL THE JOURNEY ←⊦«

IDENTIFY YOUR ARROWS

Write down activities you do that you get lost in. Describe times when you catch yourself smiling or feeling a deep sense of peace. Then go back and write down where you are when you feel this way. How much time do you spend doing these things? Is there anything you can do to add more of these moments to your life?

Notice the experiences and ideas that make you come alive. Note when you feel at home—not always in a physical sense but in terms of the things that *resonate like home* to your spirit.

JOURNEY FROM THOUGHTS TO PRAYERS

I encourage you to take those thoughts, those ideas, those dreams you've just written down and turn them into prayers. Ask God to give you direction, to show you the arrows. Start talking to Him about what you're thinking and feeling. Begin to look for ways that God could turn possibilities into reality. Will you begin praying about starting your own business or changing your lifestyle? Finding a way to slow down or reconnect with a family member?

PRAY FOR WISDOM

Growing up, after we said a blessing over our meal at the dinner table, we would say the Serenity Prayer together.

> *God, grant me the serenity*
> *to accept the things I cannot change,*
> *the courage to change the things I can,*
> *and the wisdom to know the difference.*

It's important to gain an understanding of what we do have control over and what we don't. God helps us discern the difference. He will help us see what to let go of and what we have the capacity to adjust, and He will give us the boldness to do so. Close your journaling time with this prayer, or write a prayer of your own to seek direction, ask for awareness of your arrows, and learn how to discern what is yours to do and not to do.

YOUR ARROWS

As I look back at the arrows from God in my life, I see how each destination, no matter how long I stayed there, was helping me get to where I am now. When I was a young girl, I loved helping my mom decorate and host gatherings. As an elementary school teacher for many years, I learned to love planning curriculum and teaching. Since my first apartment, in every home I've lived in, I've loved decorating and styling spaces for my family. These are just a few of the arrows I've followed.

Which way are your arrows pointing? What do they say? What destinations and stops along the way have helped prepare you for where you are now and where you may be headed?

What lies ahead of you is an amazing adventure. Whether you are gazing over the precipice or standing at a fork in the road, I want to encourage you to embrace the pure wonder of what is to come. You will be amazed at what you are capable of—even in the hard times, slow times, and stick-it-out, hold-on-to-hope times—because there is so much joy coming.

BLAZE A TRAIL

CREATE A WISDOM AND VISION BOARD

Start a vision board, wall, or book. Begin writing down ideas, tearing out magazine photos, and printing out quotes that you can hang up or glue in. You'll begin to see how the seemingly random things that inspire you all come together. It will give you a visual to keep you inspired and motivated.

I love to add to my board verses of wisdom and hope along with comments and letters of encouragement from family and friends. On the days when a dream feels very far away, glancing at inspiring words will remind you to keep going.

Add a calendar with some to-dos to move you forward, even small steps. The addition of one of your checklists would be great, and as you check things off, you will build on your successes.

Share your visions with me. I'd love to cheer you on and send you something to add to your board.

WISDOM ALONG THE WAY

*Let perseverance finish its work so that you may be
mature and complete, not lacking anything.*

JAMES 1:4

*Therefore, if anyone is in Christ, the new creation
has come: The old has gone, the new is here!*

2 CORINTHIANS 5:17

*He reached down from on high and took hold of
me; he drew me out of deep waters.*

PSALM 18:16

NORTHWOODS CONNECTION

Many of those white arrow signs in the Northwoods point to restaurants known as supper clubs. Supper clubs are only open in the evening and have a special atmosphere without the exclusivity of traditional clubs. Everyone is welcome at a supper club. They are family friendly. Decor is often cozy. They may have a roaring fireplace, white table linens, and fine china. The evening starts with an old-fashioned drink, then a relish tray to snack on at the table along with veggies, cheese and crackers, or a cranberry salsa dip. Each supper club's relish tray is unique to the restaurant. Dinner is meant to be lingered over, whether it's the tradition of a Friday night fish fry, a prime rib Saturday, or clever favorites for other days of the week. A favorite supper club dessert is a piled-high ice cream drink.

TRY THIS: SUPPER CLUB

Start your own supper club tradition. Go out to a favorite spot once a week with family and friends. Leave your phones in the car or under your seat. Linger, listen, and laugh.

Or invite a group of incredibly encouraging friends over. Pick a theme or something you have in common. Maybe you can start a cookbook club where everyone brings a dish to share from the same cookbook, or enjoy homemade pizza and then craft together. I promise you will look forward to these ways of building community that deepen friendships and stretch you to try new things. When you create community around something you love by inviting others to share in it, you not only chase your own arrows but encounter kindred spirits for your journey.

NORTHERN LIGHTS

I praise you because I am fearfully and wonderfully made;
your works are wonderful, I know that full well.

PSALM 139:14

One night a few years ago, I was driving home from a friend's house when the entire sky in front of me turned bright green. The incredible color rose and spread as if cans of paint had been spilled heavenward. I was new to life in the Northwoods, so it took me a second to realize that I was witnessing the breathtaking aurora borealis.

What's even more breathtaking is that the very same God who makes the beautiful and awe-inspiring northern lights is the God who made each of us unique and lovely. He had a plan when He made you and me—a plan that would bring Him glory and light up our lives and the lives of those around us. He wants us to live a life that shines by using our gifts from Him to the fullest.

But what if we don't know what that life looks like? What if we have dreams but don't know how to get there? What if things have changed so much that we feel completely lost?

If I met you for lunch and asked, "What makes you special?" would you avoid eye contact and stare down at your salad? Would you struggle to answer? Then this is exactly where we need to start.

Do you get how amazing you are? That you are loved, valued, and miraculously made? Created for great and unique things? God knows how marvelous you are. If you ever question your beauty and worth, read all of Psalm 139 and reflect on the declaration that we have each been skillfully woven, knitted together.

God wants each of us to experience a deep connection with ourselves, with others, and with Him. So He gave you, and me, and all His children special gifts and abilities.

Many of the reasons we think we're "not enough" actually come from the things God can use most. Doubt and discouragement arise when we're looking back at roads we wish we hadn't taken or are focusing on today's worries instead of looking upward for our identity and for the light God shines on the arrows showing us the way forward.

When I saw the northern lights that evening, I called my family right away. They ran out onto the dock so they could see the illuminated night sky and gaze in wonder.

If we want to get the full view of what God wants to show us, you and I need to step out in faith and look ahead. He has something to show us, to tell us.

HOW DO WE SEE AND HEAR GOD?

One of the first questions people have as they embark on a journey toward a dream is how to know when a plan is God's plan and not merely their own wishes and wants. Here are ways to discern God's voice in our lives.

Pray for direction. Ask God questions and share your fears and insecurities. Ask Him to show you the way. Feeling unsure? He already knows how you feel, but praying through your worries will help you get them out of your head so you can analyze if there is truth to them.

Turn up the volume on praise. Worship music is one of the ways I hear Him speak. The songs are full of reminders of His promises. It's hard to worry when you worship—when you draw your heart closer to that of your Creator, you are better able to listen and recognize what you are hearing, sensing, and discovering in this journey.

Search His Word. Look online for verses related to topics on your mind and the areas of life in which you need encouragement. Most of our worries and questions already have been asked and answered in the Bible. If you want to immerse yourself more deeply, choose a book of the Bible and prayerfully ask God for His wisdom in your life as you read and meditate on the verses.

Get quiet and listen. We can't hear God if we are doing all the talking. When we get still, He can speak to us through our thoughts, through others, and through Scripture. I talk to God throughout the entire day, but I also schedule time in my day to be alone with Him. I have found that early morning, before the rest of the house is awake, works best for me. I'm not naturally an early bird. I must be intentional about this commitment and make it a priority. What time in your day would allow you to consistently meet with and be still before God?

IF WE WANT TO GET THE FULL VIEW OF WHAT GOD WANTS TO SHOW US, YOU AND I NEED TO STEP OUT IN FAITH AND LOOK AHEAD. HE HAS SOMETHING TO SHOW US, TO TELL US.

SHINE A LIGHT ON THE STORIES OF OTHERS

God not only interacts with us personally, but He also reveals His faithfulness through the lives of others—past and present. The Bible is full of stories of people finding their way to God's purpose while on a journey. They obediently went about each day "doing their thing." Meanwhile, God was planning. And eventually, God would come to them—right where they were—when He needed them. Usually, it was a surprise visit!

Moses spent years in Midian shepherding his father-in-law Jethro's sheep. He had fled Egypt and his lifestyle as a prince, where he was surrounded by luxury. Now he was living in the desert, surrounded by desolation and sheep.

On this journey, Moses saw a burning bush that was not being consumed by the flames. He drew closer to see what was going on. In his 40 years, he had never seen anything like this.

God called to him from the bush, and Moses answered, "Here I am."

God told Moses His plan to free the Hebrews from the Egyptians and said, "Go! I'm sending you!"

Moses's response is exactly what ours tends to be: "Who, me? Who am I?"

Our list of reasons why we can't do what we dream can be long. We see lots of obstacles in the way. Moses had some too. For example, he stuttered (Exodus 4:10).

God continued to reassure Moses that He would be with him. That promise extends to us too.

SHINE A LIGHT ON YOUR STORY

Do you, like Moses, feel unqualified for what you sense God calling you to do? Are you intimidated by or even terrified of the plan God is mapping out?

Take comfort in knowing that while Moses had been tending sheep all those years, God was preparing him for what he would eventually be asked to do.

The journey you have been on, with all its seeming detours or missteps, is the journey God has been using to prepare you. The hard things, the boring

things, the times you failed, the times you learned—all of it will be used for good; it will have a purpose.

Take some time to find photos of yourself as you were growing up. Choose one from elementary school, high school, college, and so on. Study the photo, and think about who you were at that age. What dreams did you have then? Do you still have them now? What would you tell your younger self? In hindsight, which difficult experiences can you appreciate, knowing they brought you to where you are today?

If Moses had a scrapbook, he would see a photo of a baby in a basket floating down the river to where Pharaoh's daughter found him. He would see how growing up in the palace taught him how to talk to a king.

He would see a photo of himself, maybe in his twenties, fleeing to Midian, where he then tended sheep for 40 long years. Tending sheep taught him the patience and "crowd control" he needed to lead God's chosen people out of Egypt and into the wilderness for 40 years.

Everything—the blessings and the hardships—God used for His purpose. He will also do this for us.

THE JOURNEY YOU HAVE BEEN ON, WITH ALL ITS SEEMING DETOURS OR MISSTEPS, IS THE JOURNEY GOD HAS BEEN USING TO PREPARE YOU.

DISCOVER THE DREAM

One of my favorite things to do is have coffee with friends. I meet up several times a week to catch up with a girlfriend or get to know someone better.

I'd like to get to know you better. Let's pretend we are sitting down to coffee together. If I asked you right now to share your dream, what would pop into your head? It does not matter the size of the dream—whether it seems silly or far-fetched. It is something you care about, so you need to give it some time to evolve or dissolve.

You may be thinking, "But what if I don't know what I want out of life? I just know that it's not what I have right now." Maybe you are worn out and frustrated. You may even have a dream, but you don't know where to start.

How do we uncover our God-given gifts and find the courage to use them? God puts dreams inside of us; He weaves them into our being to help us find joy, develop our skills, and bring glory to Him. It starts by being aware of what our gifts are.

GIVE YOURSELF PERMISSION + GRACE

Sometimes our dreams are intimidating as well as exciting, and we become hesitant because we worry that we can't really reach them. But whether our dreams are big or small, like *Goldilocks and the Three Bears*, when we decide to work toward them, they end up just right.

The biggest decision is to make time to think about our dreams, what motivates us, and what is keeping us from starting. We need to determine which feelings are rational and which are not. One way I try to distinguish this is by asking myself, "What do I know is true?"

For example, one of our fears may be "My family and friends will think I'm crazy." But that is probably not true—they may think you are amazing and

be impressed with your courage and wish that they could be more like you. Instead of presuming people have negative assumptions, we need to change our mindset and our self-talk to be positive.

We need to give ourselves permission to dream. Later, we may decide that our dream is not a good one or the timing is not right—but we must give ourselves the time to think about it, pray, and then either shut the door or walk through it.

You must also give yourself grace and allow yourself to get excited. Don't let chapters from your past where you may not have achieved your goals cast a shadow on today. Learn from the past, but don't focus on it. There's a reason your rearview mirror is smaller than the windshield.

HOW TO START

I greet my followers online each day with "Morning, Sunshine!" With God, every sunrise brings another day to wake up and continue our journey, begin something new, or start over. We can look for direction and growth in our lives each day. I heard it said once that God isn't the God of second chances. He's the God of a brand-new life.

JOURNAL THE JOURNEY

- What gifts do you believe God gave you?

- What have people always complimented you on?

- What activities or services do you participate in that truly bring you joy?

Our days and decisions count. We don't want to wake up years from now regretting not trying something.

One of the bad habits I have is what I call "on Monday." I tend to believe initiating something new or making a change needs to start on a new day or a new week, so I push it off rather than begin right away. Planning to start on a certain day can be a good kickoff, but it can also turn into procrastinating.

The biggest challenge for most of us is to *begin*. We can spend too much time thinking about a goal and never take any action. It's fun to stay in the "planning stage," but at some point, we must act and take a step forward. What small steps can you take toward your goal today?

It may be to make one phone call, listen to one podcast, sign up for a class, or set your alarm for five in the morning. Take a blank calendar, and write a task or behavior change on each day that would move you closer to your dream.

TAKE LITTLE STEPS

When I opened my brick-and-mortar shop, one of my goals was to get all our inventory online so that my followers could shop from wherever they lived. With thousands of items in the store, this was a monumental task. I wanted to have it done within a year, so I wrote out the direct steps that I would need to take to get it accomplished. The first thing I wrote down was to hire some help. I needed to build a team to accomplish this big goal and get the results I wanted.

My goal was accomplished in less time than planned. The key was to break down the giant task into small, doable steps each day. It doesn't matter the size of your dream or your steps toward it. Sometimes the goals we make and the dreams we chase need to start small.

Doing the small things is like gathering kindling to build a fire. We need to have enough to get the flame going as well as to sustain it. We also need to have reserves in our woodshed. Every day, we can gather new ideas, learn new skills, and look for encouraging people to be around. Begin to stack your pile and fill your shed.

SHIFT YOUR LANGUAGE TOWARD POSSIBILITY

Our lakeside log cabin home started out as a vacation getaway. After about a year of visiting on weekends, we started to notice that when we were leaving to go back home on Sundays, we were all sad. We wondered if the slower

pace, focus on family, and time in nature could become a full-time reality. That's when my husband and I started to discuss the dream to move and live primarily at the lake house. Those initial conversations gave us time to think. But the idea really began to turn toward reality when we shifted the language from "Wish we could" to "What if we did?"

You may notice that your language has already changed from "wish" to "what if" on its own. Pay attention to what your heart and mind might already be telling you. Once we allowed that leap to "what if," we gave ourselves permission to explore first the small steps and then the bigger steps needed to make this dream a reality.

A few months after our initial conversations, a lot of prayer, and the "Let's do it" from our five kids, we made the move.

You can use the same change in wording with your goals and dreams. Maybe your dream is to add a relaxing hobby to your life. Instead of saying, "I wish I could knit," you can say, "What if I learned to knit?" It takes the dream from an inactive option to an exciting possibility. The "what if" leads to joy—if we just try.

I have discovered how this practice of changing one word or one phrase can greatly transform my thought patterns and my mindset. For example, instead of saying, "I *have to go* to the store," I say, "I *get to go* to the store." It turns it from a negative to a positive, from a chore to a blessing. Think of other phrases that you could change to give your attitude a shift and move yourself into action.

IT DOESN'T MATTER THE SIZE OF YOUR DREAM OR YOUR STEPS TOWARD IT. SOMETIMES THE GOALS WE MAKE AND THE DREAMS WE CHASE NEED TO START SMALL.

OUR GUIDING LIGHT

Are you afraid to identify a dream and chase after it? Full disclosure: This journey we're on may very well start a new chapter in your life. And new chapters in life can certainly bring challenges and the discomfort of change; however, they also usher in wonderful possibilities. My daughter has a sign hanging in her room that says, "I trust the next chapter because I know the author." My husband and I always talk about the changes in our lives as "just the next chapter" in our story. As the kids grow older, we are nostalgic for the past but embrace the present and look forward to the future. Each chapter is different but keeps us excited to see what will happen next on the adventure. We can have confidence because we can trust God's guiding light and know that it's His hand creating our guiding arrows.

What will your next chapter be? It may involve taking steps to appreciate where you are right now. It might invite you to make a small change to connect more deeply with your spouse. You may be dreaming about something big and need encouragement and advice for a small next step. Or maybe you face your first year as an empty nester and are wondering what that means for you, your purpose, and the nudge of a dream.

Moses saw quite a light show in that burning bush, and so did I in the night sky. You might not be able to look up at the northern lights where you live, and you might not encounter a burning bush, but God is trying to get your attention. He is revealing Himself in light and beauty in your own journey. Be sure to look up and look around. You don't want to miss an expression of His love and His hope for your life.

BLAZE A TRAIL
SET UP A QUIET SPACE

Setting up a quiet-time space can truly bless you. Find inspiration in these tips for styling a spot that encourages you and allows room *physically* to open you up mentally for noticing, dreaming, discerning, and even planning those small next steps.

- Find a corner or surface that you can leave always set up.
- Designate a favorite chair, or move in a small desk.
- Add a lamp, a candle, your journal, your Bible, and a pen.
- Stack a few of your favorite books.
- Keep a throw blanket nearby.
- Set out a frame with an encouraging quote or verse.
- Have a coaster or end table to hold a glass or mug.
- If you don't have space, then find a basket or tote bag that you can bring with you.

WISDOM ALONG THE WAY

And who knows but that you have come to your
royal position for such a time as this?

ESTHER 4:14

"For I know the plans I have for you," declares the LORD, "plans to
prosper you and not to harm you, plans to give you hope and a future."

JEREMIAH 29:11

But the plans of the LORD stand firm forever, the
purposes of his heart through all generations.

PSALM 33:11

NORTHWOODS CONNECTION

Many cottages and cabins in the Northwoods have been in families for generations. There are camps still in existence that travelers have been coming to for a lifetime. There are also some families who are new to the area, beginning a legacy. I love listening to the nostalgic memories people share and finding out what traditions they try to continue today. These stories are so intriguing to me: The place is important—the lake, cottage, cabin, or camp. But most of all, the stories are about the people they come just to see and who they love and remember time with so fondly. Special relationships like these help you know one another in meaningful ways. Those long conversations around the campfire. The lingering breakfasts around the table. The day out on the boat fishing together. These times connect us deeply.

TRY THIS: CONNECT WITH A FRIEND

Take a trusted friend or family member out for coffee, and share your journal thoughts from this chapter with them. Ask them if they see the same things you see or if they see something different from what you shared. This can reinforce what you are feeling or even give you a new direction. Pass on the encouragement. Open up and give them a compliment on how you have been blessed by a gift you see in them.

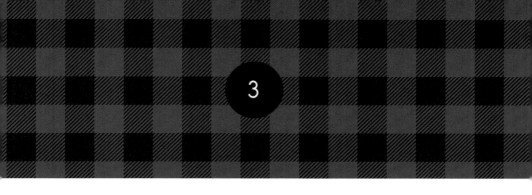

WHERE THE GRASS
IS GREENER

Wait for the LORD; be strong and take heart and wait for the LORD.

PSALM 27:14

I'm a quote collector. I gravitate toward books full of them. As I hear or see new ones that inspire me, I write the insights down in journals, screenshot the words on my phone, and pin the wisdom to my office wall. A few years ago, I saw this quote: "The grass is greener where you water it."

I sat and let that one sink in for a while. It gave clarity and words to something I have always believed. And it has continued to give me encouragement ever since.

The grass (life) is not always greener (better) on the other side; we may just need to water it (life) where we are. Sometimes, instead of looking for the next new thing, we should nurture what we have and where we are. This is true in all areas of life: personally, professionally, relationally, physically, and spiritually.

How can we put positive energy into our families, friendships, and marriages to help them thrive? In our work or home, how can we enrich our situation just by shifting our attitude and mindset? Are there dreams you are already living but haven't had time to realize because stress or busyness has taken over?

FINDING CONTENTMENT

I've been known to love dreaming and planning so much that my brain stays focused on what's next, what I wish was happening, or where I would prefer to be. When I'm fixated on what isn't happening, then I am not noticing or enjoying what I have and what I'm doing in the present moment.

Sometimes the dreams and anticipatory thoughts can pile up and make us feel a bit lost. As we try to figure out why we feel lost, we can assume that a big change is the catalyst necessary to feel better. Yet I've realized most of us will feel less lost when we stop searching and embrace contentment in the here and now. Before we can be certain a big change is needed, we must become comfortable with who we are, right where we are, and then we can make decisions from a place of wisdom and discernment rather than impulsiveness.

Contentment is such a treasure. You will recognize it when you uncover it. It is feeling right at home, calm without worry or anxiety—at peace with ourselves, with what we are doing, and where we are doing it.

Do you feel it? Are you searching for it?

I believe it starts simply—with gratitude.

> MOST OF US WILL FEEL LESS LOST WHEN WE STOP SEARCHING AND EMBRACE CONTENTMENT IN THE HERE AND NOW.

APPRECIATE WHAT YOU HAVE

There is a lot written about counting blessings. But the potential of this is too powerful not to mention here as well. When I start feeling myself get overwhelmed, I start mentally ticking off everything I can think of that I'm thankful for. No matter how small or how big, I bring them to mind.

It's almost impossible to name everything. Once I start, my attitude changes for the better, gradually lifting as my list grows. Before I know it, I've brought myself back into balance. I'm able to get a fresh perspective.

Some people keep a gratitude journal. I love the idea of this, and even though I'm a writer, I have never gotten into the practice. Maybe it's time to try again—time to finish each day by picking up a journal in the evening and writing about what I'm thankful for.

To nurture gratitude as a regular habit, keep a running list in your phone's notes as you think of blessings throughout the day. Simply offer up a prayer as a thank you comes to mind.

One practice I've started over the past few years is to write someone a thank-you note, message, or email every day. I keep a stack of pretty notecards on my desk where just the sight of them is a reminder to think of others and reach out to them. One note might go out to a coworker or one of my kids' teachers. I sent one to the journalist who always writes such great articles about my daughter's sports teams in the local paper. One went to the postal express in town where the staff is always so kind and helpful. Sending out these small messages of gratitude ends up helping me feel uplifted too.

APPRECIATE WHERE YOU ARE

Take some time to sit and reflect on your location. Where do you live? Are you a country mouse or a city mouse? Still in your hometown or far away from family? How did you end up where you are?

Understanding our story's setting is important. The dot on the map that we call home can bring us a lot of joy; sometimes we may just have to go looking for it. You may not live in your ideal locale, and you may feel stuck there without options, but there are ways to embrace it.

Here are some simple ways to appreciate where you live and be in the moment:

- When you are the passenger in the car, put your phone down and look out the window.
- Notice ten beautiful things on your drive to work or the grocery store.
- Visit locally owned businesses when you need a gift, something new to wear, or something for your home.
- Frequent your town's parks, and eat lunch there on a sunny day.
- Walk in your neighborhood or on a local trail. Maybe try a different trail each week until you discover a favorite.
- Shop at the local farmers market.

There are so many fun ways to explore your town. Once you begin to discover activities to do and places to see, I know your list of local joys will keep growing. Pretend you are a tourist, and research what restaurants, attractions, and events are recommended.

WATER YOUR RELATIONSHIPS

We can deepen our friendships, growing the roots and building a support system around us that brings joy and fun into our lives as well as help and encouragement.

Each of us has different social needs. Based on our personalities or the circumstances and season of life, we may prefer to lean into the support and intimacy of a small group of dear friends or prefer a much larger network of different friend groups. Some of us may still be connected to friends from our

past, even though we don't live close anymore. Our best friends may be from our own family.

For example, take that coffee date I love to have with a dear friend or new one: It's a simple ask, it's easy to fit into my schedule and theirs, and it's budget friendly. I gather with one group of friends once a week at a coffee shop in town. We have time to talk about our kids and life's happenings, and we support a local small business.

The ways to share time with friends are endless. Choose activities or settings you and they love or are interested in adding to your lives. Go for a walk or attend a workout class together. If you have similar interests, start a group centered on those interests. A book club or craft night can strengthen the ties between you and others. Imagine what would give you joy each time the get-together appears on your calendar. Take time to tend to and water those relationships you want to see thrive.

SEE THE GOOD

If we focus on the negative—the grumpy cashier, the car that cut us off, and so on—we will see more negative. But the more we watch for good, the better the view we will see.

One day, I was walking across the parking lot toward the grocery store. A couple was walking together a little way in front of me. Suddenly, a car pulled into the drive without stopping for them. The man was irate. He screamed at the car. He kept crabbing all the way into the store. I was so focused on his negativity that I started to feel a bit grumpy myself—until I remembered to look for the good.

Guess what I saw? An abundance of kindness, helpfulness, and generosity as I went around and filled my cart. If I had stayed agitated and distracted by the negative encounter, I would've missed witnessing people smiling, offering to put away carts, or letting someone else go ahead of them in line.

Negativity can be big and powerful. Have you noticed how easily you gloss

over the several compliments you receive in a day but are fixated on the solitary negative comment? I refuse to give a small bit of bad news more attention than it deserves. I have a box to hold cards people have written to me or sweet comments they've sent in. I keep adding to this treasure trove of encouragement. If I have one of those days, I open the box and sift through the sweet reminders that there's more good than bad in the world. If we keep looking for the good, we will find it and see more of it.

"I remain confident of this: I will see the goodness of the LORD" (Psalm 27:13). When I looked up this verse in my Bible to reference it for this chapter, I saw I had starred and dated it in October a couple years ago. I love highlighting, underlining, dating, and putting notes in my Bible. It's like looking back at a scrapbook of photos with old friends.

At that time, I was going through some trying parenting moments with one of our kids and the choices they were making. Verses like these gave me so much encouragement, and now when I look back, I can see God's provision throughout that season.

JOURNAL THE JOURNEY

- What is one relationship that comes to mind when you think about reconnecting or deepening the roots of friendship? Why is this important to you?

- Spend some time searching Bible verses. Choose one that stands out to you. Write it out, and describe why it's speaking to you at this time.

- What is something you love about where you live?

Those verses were singled out for something I was going through at that time or something I was learning. I can look back in awe of where I've come from or how I've grown. Sometimes those verses still speak to me deeply and I need to keep them close again.

IN THE WAITING

It isn't always clear whether God is telling us to make a big change, stay where we are, or wait a bit longer. A life-changing lesson I've learned about times of uncertainty is that they may indicate not a *yes* or *no* in our circumstance, but a *not yet*.

When in such a season, I've found peace and contentment by finding ways to rejuvenate myself personally, professionally, and spiritually. If this is where you are right now, be encouraged. The "not yet" times create the most fertile ground for growth when we are intentional about what we water and what we nurture.

After the Hebrews left Egypt, they journeyed in the wilderness for 40 years in rough conditions before entering the Promised Land. They were wandering and waiting, waiting and wandering. During the waiting, God provided them with what they needed. In Exodus 16:15, Moses explains that God is providing "bread from heaven," called manna, each morning for them to eat. In your waiting, God will provide for your needs too.

THE "NOT YET" TIMES CREATE THE MOST FERTILE GROUND FOR GROWTH WHEN WE ARE INTENTIONAL ABOUT WHAT WE WATER AND WHAT WE NURTURE.

WHAT'S INSIDE

I heard it said once that when we get "bumped" (by some frustration or hard time), what's inside us comes out. Think of us like buckets of water. We've all seen this in our families, friends, coworkers, other people driving down the road, people at the store, even ourselves. Who have you seen that, when "bumped," seems to spill out something full of hope, honesty, and goodness rather than anger and blame?

That's why what we fill ourselves with matters so much—it's what will come back out. Proverbs 23:7 says, "For as he thinketh in his heart, so is he" (KJV).

It matters what we listen to, what we read, what we watch. It matters what we spend time on and who we spend time with.

If we want to lead a flourishing life, then we need to fill ourselves with things that encourage us, teach us, challenge us, and help us move forward.

There are so many amazing podcasts and books available. We have easy access to leaders and teachers through videos and courses. We can find mentors we may never even meet in person who can enrich and stretch us. We must make a conscious effort to choose those things.

REJUVENATE PERSONALLY

When I think about rejuvenating, I think of practices and activities that help me unwind and rest but also things that make me stronger.

I heard it said once that if you work with your hands, you should rest with your mind. If you work with your mind, rest with your hands.

Do you sit at a desk during the week spending time typing, selling, and talking? You may find your best rest in quiet work in the garden or crafting. If you spend your days caring for patients in the hospital, you may enjoy getting lost in a great novel or taking quiet walks.

There are several things I know I can do to restore myself. This wisdom comes from years of learning more about myself and my needs. I'm a very social person, but I also need alone time. My alone time fills me back up. If I don't set margins for solitude, I handle everything else in life a bit tippy and off-balance. I'm not centered enough to be discerning or intentional.

Is there something you crave more of? Are you missing an activity or creative practice you used to enjoy but have forgotten to bring into your current life? One of my friends shared with me about being in a community leadership group. They were going to be working together for a year to bring forward a project to better their town while growing as leaders as well. During the first gathering, they were asked to share about a time when they were flourishing. She said the question brought tears to her eyes because she hadn't realized how much she missed running. As her career and life had become busier, time devoted to running had been pushed out of her schedule. The next week, she started training for a marathon. Putting running back into her regular schedule transformed her days and her hope.

Exercise is high on my list as well. When I have a consistent workout schedule, I feel so much better, and it impacts other areas of my life. Like a lot of interests and activities, it can often be put on the back burner, so I must protect it as a priority. You may have noticed it takes a long time to get into a routine and only a short time to get out of it!

Getting enough sleep is also high on my list. So is trying to make wise decisions about what I put into my body. Over the years, I've done all kinds of diets, eating plans, and fasting routines, but I've found the sweet spot in asking myself just one question over and over: "Will this nourish me?" Breaking it down into a yes-or-no question keeps it simple. For example, if it's real, farm-fresh food and will nourish me, hydrate me, and fuel me, it's a yes. If it's processed, then I try to say no.

Music is something else that really refreshes me. Having it on in the background during the day, listening to it as I work out, singing along as I drive in the car—music replenishes.

If I need a quick boost of rejuvenation when I'm feeling overwhelmed, frazzled, or busy, if I can give myself 20 to 30 minutes, I try one of the following:

putting in my earbuds, lying on my bed, and closing my eyes

going for a walk

grabbing a stack of magazines to flip through

pouring an iced coffee or kombucha and sitting in a rocking chair on the porch

A foundational personal priority in my life is to stay renewed spiritually. Spending time in prayer and meditation is a focus; so are Scripture reading, Bible study, and journaling. Waking up early gives me the extra time I need to protect this priority.

REJUVENATE PROFESSIONALLY

In my professional life, one of the things that I find most helpful is to read books and listen to podcasts that I can learn from and find encouragement in. I try to read a book a month that enriches my professional life. Maybe one month, it's on leadership; another, on time management; and another, on listening and conversation.

Another activity that helps me is spending time with my team talking through ideas and getting their feedback. One of my priorities when I opened my shop was to surround myself with an amazing staff who are not only great at what they do but positive, encouraging, and fun. This makes our weekly meetings and time together in the shop enriching. I grow and learn from them as I listen to their ideas and advice.

For me, I also get a lot of rejuvenation out of traveling, even if it's just a day exploring, an overnight, or a weekend. Eating new foods, seeing how hotel lobbies are decorated, and shopping in downtown areas all give me ideas to take back home.

Believe it or not, doing my work invigorates me for my work. If I get uninterrupted time to write, it is pure bliss for me. Taking a "retreat" for myself, even by working at home for the day, can let me find joy in the process when I have deadlines or big ideas to work through.

Setting up my workspace to be comfortable and special is also uplifting for me. I spent time this past year setting up a new office space at my shop—the way I had been dreaming of it. I finished off the upstairs bonus space (a back building with wood paneling), then added cute lighting and my favorite accessories. I split the space into three zones: One is for gathering with coworkers or clients. There's a small sofa, a table, chairs, and a coffee bar. Another zone is for podcasting, where our equipment can be left out all the time rather than boxed up after each recording session. The third zone has my desk. I like to work spread out, with stacks of the projects I'm working on around me, so I found a great dining table to be my desk.

At home I've done the same thing, setting up a workspace in the loft of our cabin.

All my spaces share a few things: a coaster for whatever beverage I like to have nearby, a lamp, a candle, a pot of pencils, and vintage items like an old typewriter and clock.

Not only do these items bring me comfort, but they also energize me because they signal to my mind that this is my workspace, my time to get busy.

DO THE THINGS

There are things that we should do right where we are. I have goals and activities that I want to do that often don't get done. Usually, the only reasons I don't start or follow through are misplaced time and priorities. For example, I think about how fun and relaxing it would be to read on the dock in the mornings. Then a week goes by, and I haven't done it. It would be so easy; it's right out the back door. If I did it, it would become a habit I know I would love. I just need to go do it.

Another activity I have always wanted to do is play tennis. For the past three years, I have known women who played, but I never made the time to buy a racket or a can of balls. But this past summer, some of the women invited me to play, and I decided to join them. I'm so glad I did! Not only is it a lot of fun, but it also gives me extra exercise and time with friends.

What is one thing you've always wanted to do but have not made the time for? How can you prioritize it in the coming weeks and let it be a part of your schedule and life?

As we work on "keeping our grass green," let's remember to do the following:

appreciate

look for good

cultivate

rejuvenate

do the things

As we see ourselves grow and our relationships deepen, we will be able to evaluate, from a healthy place, whether we are right where we need to be. And by being intentional and "watering" where we are at, we can find our calling and purpose right there.

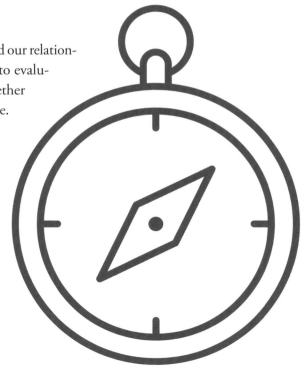

BLAZE A TRAIL
GATHER INSPIRING MESSAGES

Choose some favorite quotes that speak to your heart and encourage you. Glue them into your journal. Snap a photo or screenshot to use as a screen saver. You can even hang a few on your fridge or bathroom mirror. I have included some of my favorites for you on the next pages. Keeping these reminders visible can keep your attitude positive and your momentum going forward.

"THE LORD WILL FIGHT FOR YOU;
YOU NEED ONLY TO BE STILL."

EXODUS 14:14

"WHEN YOU GO THROUGH DEEP
WATERS. I WILL BE WITH YOU."

ISAIAH 43:2 NLT

"FOR WITH GOD NOTHING
SHALL BE IMPOSSIBLE."

LUKE 1:37 KJV

"GOD IS WITHIN HER;
SHE WILL NOT FALL."

PSALM 46:5

"I CAN DO ALL THINGS THROUGH
CHRIST WHO STRENGTHENS ME."

PHILIPPIANS 4:13 NKJV

"THEREFORE ENCOURAGE ONE
ANOTHER AND BUILD EACH OTHER UP."

1 THESSALONIANS 5:11

"RISE UP...
TAKE COURAGE AND DO IT."

EZRA 10:4

"GRACE UPON GRACE."

JOHN 1:16 ESV

WISDOM ALONG THE WAY

*The L*ORD *will guide you always;*
he will satisfy your needs in a sun-scorched land
and will strengthen your frame.
You will be like a well-watered garden,
like a spring whose waters never fail.

ISAIAH 58:11

*Be strong and take heart, all you who hope in the L*ORD.

PSALM 31:24

Blessed is she who has believed that the Lord would fulfill his promises to her!

LUKE 1:45

NORTHWOODS CONNECTION

On our first trip up north, we pulled into a restaurant surrounded by towering pines with a creek meandering past out back. It was a ramshackle log cabin that looked straight out of a Northwoods postcard. As we got out of the vehicle, I was stopped still by the enveloping fresh air surrounding us. Now, I hadn't come from a dirty city, but this was still such a refreshing surprise. It smelled like being high up in the mountains—that mix of timber, pine, and water. It was energizing.

TRY THIS: FAVORITE FRAGRANCES

Find some favorite fragrances that calm, energize, or restore you, and then fill your spaces with them. These pleasant scents will make you feel peaceful and happy to be where you are. You may enjoy using essential oils and a diffuser. Here are a few ideas to do right on your stovetop.

For each combination, just fill a pot with water, set it on the stove, and simmer.

2 whole lemons, sliced	2 whole limes, sliced	5 cinnamon sticks
2 sprigs rosemary	3 sprigs thyme	1 tsp. vanilla extract
1 T. vanilla extract	1 tsp. vanilla extract	4 bay leaves
	handful of fresh mint	1½ T. whole cloves
		a few orange slices

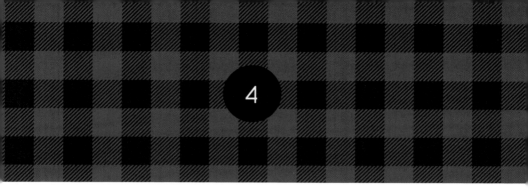

SWEET SPOTS

Let me hear in the morning of your steadfast love, for in you I trust.
Make me know the way I should go.

PSALM 143:8 ESV

Where are you most at peace? Where can you find quiet? Our world continues to be noisy and so, so busy. We must be intentional about finding quiet or creating places to experience it.

When we first bought our cabin, we made trips up north nearly every weekend. After a few weeks, we noticed a consistent moment along the drive when we knew we hit the Northwoods. Yes, we could see the four-lane highway turn into two lanes and the birch and pine trees become thicker in form, but the wonder was that we sensed it as well. We felt our blood pressure drop. Our breathing would slow down, as if the increased greenery was immediately expanding our oxygen reserves and giving us new life. I began calling this area the "sweet spot."

Where are your sweet spots? Where are you in your element, and where do you feel the most alive? I bet these are places you think about a lot and wish you could visit often. They may be somewhere you travel to, or they may be in your home. Hopefully, you can identify some places that are easy for you to access without much effort.

Some of my favorite sweet spots are our local ice cream shop as well as my own shop, White Arrows Home—especially when my friend does her pop-up to sell her homemade pies. Okay, I know…these spots offer literal sweetness, but what I'm really talking about are the moments that are sweet—where you feel alive and are doing what you feel you were created to do. This often happens when you are doing an activity or are in a location where you lose track of time, and suddenly you think, "How did an hour already go by?"

When we lose ourselves in something, we can discover a deeper connection to our purpose and passions. In those sweet spots, we make room that allows us to hear God's direction and tune in to inner joy.

SUNRISE TO SUNSET

Starting and ending our days with planned times of quiet can help bring more of that sweet peace to our hearts and our human experience. When you build in healthy habits from sunrise to sunset—creating space for stillness, wellness, and openness to what God has to tell you—you will create spiritual and physical balance. You will prepare your heart for the decisions you face and the dreams you are pursuing and nurturing.

Where in your schedule and life can you make space for quiet? Are there places you can go to be still and alone? Maybe it's the spot we talked about creating in chapter 1. Finding this time and these spaces opens room for new ideas, dreams, and plans to emerge.

Our family moved to the Northwoods to have more time at our collective sweet spot—where we all found the most peace. You may not need to make such a dramatic move. You may just need to carve out an hour, a day, a weekend, or a week somewhere that is restful and rejuvenates your soul.

To consider your sweet spots and the times and places where you can be alone with God, first tap into the feelings you have in certain settings, environments,

and landscapes or even at specific times of the day. Scan the past few weeks, months, and years to identify points of aliveness and times when you felt God's leading in visceral ways.

WHEN WE LOSE OURSELVES IN SOMETHING, WE CAN DISCOVER A DEEPER CONNECTION TO OUR PURPOSE AND PASSIONS.

Tuning in to those feelings will help you hone in on future ways to flourish. Follow the feelings and assurances leading to a small change you can make tomorrow, and be willing to keep following them over time. Become aware of those habits and sweet spots that require longer seasons of preparation, some new learning, or even bigger changes.

GOOD MORNING, SUNSHINE

Downtime may be what I crave the most in my life. It rejuvenates me. I know that I need quiet times to move an idea forward. With a busy family and schedule, you may (like me) only have the option to get up earlier or stay up later to get that space.

My tendency, over the years, was to be a night owl and work between 11:00 p.m. and 2:00 a.m. while my family slept. Words and creativity would flow out of me with ease in these peaceful hours. But as I got older, the late nights started leaving me feeling groggy the next day. So I decided to become an early bird. (I've always admired you early birds!) What motivated me to get up earlier was to write out a schedule that starts my day at five in the morning. It includes to-dos like hydrating as soon as I wake up, doing a stretching session, and taking a quick shower with a few minutes of cold water at the end to wake up every cell in my body and brain. I am encouraged to continue making this practice a priority as I read and hear more about its numerous health benefits and discover them in my own mind and body.

I encourage you to give early mornings a try. After you wake up, grab a cup of tea or coffee and your Bible, devotional, or prayer journal. Head to that special corner or favorite chair or out to the porch. I like to go to the dock when the weather permits. Doing this can give you the chance to hear God and be more prepared to live authentically in your personal direction.

Having time to fill my body with good things and think about ideas, dreams, and even problems clears my head so I can be more focused on my husband and children when they wake up. It has been one of the best ways I've found to combat rushing when the day starts. When I commit to this personal time, I give my family a more peaceful mom and wife.

If you are not a morning person, think about how you currently spend your first waking hours and compare this to how you wish they were spent. What would your ideal morning look like? Use my plan or make your own, then try it out for one week, focusing on good habits one morning at a time. Intentionality for our day starts right away each morning. As for the days that don't go as planned, we can find peace in knowing our gracious God gives us a new morning the next day to begin again.

Here's an example of my morning routine, where I dedicate a few hours to fill myself with things that are positive and encouraging:

5:00   wake up
       drink a glass of water with sea salt and the juice of one lemon
       start a cup of tea
       do a five-minute stretch routine while the tea steeps
       if the weather permits, head outside to drink my tea, pray, and get some
          sunlight
5:30   read my devotions, study the Bible, journal
6:15   do brain-work exercises
6:30   walk, run, or spin (I do strength training in the afternoon after work)

7:30   shower (last three minutes with cold water)

8:00   get ready while listening to a speaker or podcast

8:30   have breakfast

I adjust this for the school year or summer, and based on my kids' schedules or times I may need to be at work earlier.

One of the most important things to do is get up as soon as the alarm goes off—no resetting, snoozing, or giving myself time to reconsider. It needs to be an instant reaction.

PEACE DURING THE DAY

Finding moments of peace during the day can really keep us on track. Whether it's a physical place that offers stillness and reflection or a space we create in our mind and spirit, in the quiet, we can sort through our thoughts better and hear God whisper to us, guiding us toward our dreams.

One of the great things about life in the Northwoods is that it is the epitome of peace. Unless my dog is barking, the UPS driver is stopping, or a boat is going by on the lake, the amount of noise I'm surrounded by is up to me. Sitting by my window right now, the only things I can hear are the leaves blowing in the breeze and the water ruffled by the wind.

But even though I live where it is peaceful, I can still fill my days with activity and hustle. So I've learned that I must be intentional about slowing down by building times of rest into my day. Here are some ideas:

Spend a peaceful half hour walking in your neighborhood.

Loosen your creativity by jogging a favorite trail.

Stop at the library to read for half an hour each day to truly be quiet. (The librarian will be there if you need reminding!)

Visit a local coffee shop, choose a table in the corner, pop in your earbuds, and pull out your book, journal, or sketchbook.

Take your dog to the dog park and play catch.

These activities are great ways to get some peace and quiet. Add in some midday moments for listening and making space to breathe and refresh. You *can* find time for them; the scheduling just needs to become part of your routine. Make these official by writing them in your calendar. You wouldn't break a lunch date with a friend, so be a friend to yourself and don't break your commitments to your sweet time with God and your thoughts.

IN THE QUIET, WE CAN SORT THROUGH OUR THOUGHTS BETTER AND HEAR GOD WHISPER TO US, GUIDING US TOWARD OUR DREAMS.

HABITS FOR A GOOD NIGHT

Investing in peaceful moments for the next day begins at the end of the current one. A slow, intentional bedtime routine that becomes a habit will get us there. Just as we don't want to rush into and throughout our day, we don't want to simply fall into bed exhausted. We need to be intentional, and over time, it will then become natural. Setting up an evening pattern can become something to look forward to, just like calm mornings.

For all of us, this can look different, based on who lives in your home and what the rest of your evening is like.

Consider how much time you need to fall asleep (not just get into bed), and then work backward. I like to try for at least seven hours of sleep at night, so to wake up at five, I need to go to sleep by ten each evening.

Our family usually gathers to watch a show in the evenings. Since my kids were little, this habit has been the start of our wind-down time.

Whether we watch a seasonal sporting event or work our way through a TV series, when our family screen time is over, everyone heads to bed or to their homework.

My evening skin-care and teeth-cleaning routine becomes reflective as I peek at the encouragements, ponderings, and verses I have attached to my mirror. The lavender peppermint scent of my favorite lotion helps me relax, as do the dim lights. I turn off overhead lights throughout the house and turn on the gentle light of lamps. In my bathroom, I often light a candle and play music. I'm setting a mood to signal to my body and mind that it's time to slow down and get ready to rest.

Because we make our bed every morning, it's a treat to pull back the covers. Just before I slip inside, I spray a lavender linen spray lightly over the pillows. Again, I only have lamps or candles on in our room at bedtime, letting my eyes adjust to sleepy-time light levels.

Want to know my trick for the nights I struggle to fall asleep? Though it is rare, occasionally I need to do this exercise. I take a visual trip to the homes I have lived in or my grandparents' homes. I start by pulling into the driveway, and then I take a "walk" through each room, "looking" around and remembering. I have never made it through a whole tour before falling asleep.

JOURNAL THE JOURNEY

- Where have you felt most content and at peace? What about it made those feelings emerge?

- Write out your current morning schedule. What are you pleased with, and what do you want to tweak? Rewrite how you'd like mornings to go.

- Write out your current evening schedule. What are you pleased with, and what do you want to tweak? Rewrite how you'd like evenings to go.

BRAVE THE QUIET

Finding more peace is worth striving for. It's worth the initial work we put into it. Some of us aren't naturally wired for this, so you may be thinking, "I don't even know what being peaceful feels like."

If our soul is restless, peace will be evasive. We won't find it in success, wealth, fame, or relationships. Filling our lives with stuff and busyness is just a way of running away. It may be that the biggest thing we are afraid of is what we will hear if we slow down and spend time with our own thoughts. Be brave enough to try the quiet. Be bold enough to explore your thoughts. Pray. On the other side, if we are audacious enough to journey through, we will find more peace.

Stillness can give us what we need more than striving, motion, and effort. It's the base to help us keep the rest of life in balance.

After Moses led the Hebrews out of Egypt, the Egyptians—all Pharaoh's horses and chariots, horsemen and troops—pursued them. The Hebrews were afraid and complained to Moses that he should have just left them as slaves in Egypt. When we are fearful, it becomes easy to doubt and complain. Let's work against that easy reaction and listen to the advice in Moses's response: "The LORD will fight for you; you need only to be still" (Exodus 14:14).

Finding moments and places of peace will open space for us to think and settle our busy brains. And as we find our sweet spots, we will find our rhythm with ease—and this journey will bring more joy.

BLAZE A TRAIL
START A PRAYER JOURNAL

Make your own prayer journal. Choose a pretty notebook or composition book to write down requests and praises. As you go back through, put a *P* with a circle around it next to those that have been answered or have changed for the better. Entries can be written-out prayers or simply just one word, a name, or a phrase. Keep a list of things you are praying for yourself, your family, and your friends. Don't forget to write down your dreams and goals and then ask God to direct your path.

Writing things down can help all the thoughts and noise in your head calm down, letting you focus on the concerns on your mind and in your heart. Seeing them on paper can give you a steady perspective. Prayer does something amazing, even in the stage of waiting for answers. It changes us and gives us more peace.

Don't forget to take time often to look back at how many items you've written a *P* next to!

WISDOM ALONG THE WAY

Because of the Lord's great love we are not consumed,
for his compassions never fail.
They are new every morning;
great is your faithfulness.

LAMENTATIONS 3:22-23

Turn from evil and do good;
seek peace and pursue it.

PSALM 34:14

Call to me and I will answer you and tell you great
and unsearchable things you do not know.

JEREMIAH 33:3

NORTHWOODS CONNECTION

The Northwoods area we live in covers two counties with more than 2,400 lakes, named and unnamed. Water is a big part of life here. We love sitting and relaxing by it and enjoying recreational activities in all seasons. During warmer months, we enjoy fishing, kayaking, waterskiing, paddleboarding, and canoeing. When the temperatures drop and the lakes freeze thick and solid, we ice-skate, snowshoe, and snowmobile across their expanse.

Being near water is not only fun but important for our bodies, helping us relax and reflect. It also lets us delight in God's creation. The awe we feel carries over into our perspective, and we trust that God shapes beauty in us too.

Where can you go to spend time near water?

TRY THIS: WATER REFRESHERS

To stay hydrated throughout the day, there are a variety of great bottle options to keep your water cool on the go. When I'm at home, using a vintage glass or goblet encourages me to keep sipping. Not only is it pretty, but it's a visual reminder that I'm worth taking care of. When out thrifting or antiquing, keep your eyes peeled for your own special cup.

For extra refreshment and a sense of pampering, add fresh herbs and fruits to your water. Infuse it (and yourself) with more vitamins and sensory delights. Here are some of my favorite flavor combinations you could try:

BLUEBERRY + BASIL

STRAWBERRY + LEMON + BASIL

ORANGE + GINGER

WATERMELON + KIWI + LIME

PINEAPPLE + MANGO + BLACKBERRY

CUCUMBER + LEMON

RASPBERRY + ROSEMARY

5

PACK THE WAGON

For he will command his angels concerning
you to guard you in all your ways.

PSALM 91:11

Our real-life travels can give us great insight into how to approach our dream journey.

When planning for a vacation, we dream of where to go, research locales, consult maps, and read blogs and articles. Every amazing adventure starts with preparation. Think back to the ideas in the previous chapters, where we laid the groundwork for this next big step and prepared our hearts and minds to take a risk, try something new, or pour more into where we already happen to be.

Just as we'd never travel without the gear we need, we can't chase a dream without developing a packing list. One that makes sure you don't forget any essentials. One that lets you know what you should bring and even what you should leave behind.

My younger daughter went to Europe for several weeks one summer. She traveled with a group of high school band students from around our state to play concerts in five different countries. We had meetings and discussions over email focused on what items the students should bring along to make their trip easier, more enjoyable, and more successful. The leaders also made sure to let them know what not to bring and what not to do because it could spoil their trip.

The same concept can apply to this journey you and I are on as we chase dreams big and small. There are ways to be more prepared so we can enjoy the adventure. We can't anticipate everything that will appear on or alter our path, but we can be sure our "suitcases" are full of supplies, strategies, and helpful hints to equip us to succeed with fewer frustrations.

SUPPLIES + EQUIPMENT

Packing: Do you dread it? Do you find yourself procrastinating so long you end up throwing things in your bag last minute? Or do you enjoy pulling all the necessary items together starting days ahead? Maybe you are an overpacker, always worrying that you won't have something you need.

Often, with our dreams, there's no specific timeline. We don't have a reservation or plane to catch, so we can take the time to gather what we need. We need to include items to help sustain us, items to motivate us, and items to help us relax and enjoy the journey. There are so many intangibles that we will need to pack, but there are also some tangibles—things we can hold on to—to keep close at hand to sustain us.

Many of the tools that motivate us, like our Bible, need to be tucked in tight. If you've started to journal or put together your vision board, you and your eagerness will be served by those tools. A batch of dynamic books may offer you insights and inspiration. Those quotes and mirror messages you accumulate will propel you forward.

Good health and supportive habits are also vital to keep tuned up and packed along. There's a lot of momentum gained from taking time to relax and enjoy the journey too. It gives us stamina through rejuvenation and recovery. Resting gives us time to reflect and helps us remember why the planning and forethought for our dreams are worth it.

So let's pack the Word, the practice of prayer, a journal, our books, and motivational messages, and let's make room for rest.

STRATEGIES + RESOURCES

One of my sons went on a 24-hour-challenge hike in the mountains of Georgia. My eyes got bigger and bigger as I learned more about what his adventure would look like. He didn't know every obstacle his team would face, but he knew it would be hard physically, mentally, and spiritually, and he prepared the best he could for it all.

He took along supplies to keep him hydrated and nourished. In his pack were items to help in any weather. And something I wouldn't have thought of—he had to really prepare to take care of his feet on an arduous trek like that, being ready for blisters and soreness and even getting his feet wet.

To prepare, he was doing a lot of reading. He listened to podcasts featuring past participants. He tried to use any resources available to stack the chances of success higher before he started.

When that same kid was around six, I took him on another adventure. This one was to a theme park that was always crowded and known for many "must-do" rides and activities. I found a blog that gave me the inside scoop on the best way to spend a day at the park. I printed the info and followed the plan. We ended up not waiting in a single line! Our journey through the park was filled with adventure. Using the strategy of someone who had gone before me saved us time and made the experience so much more fun and memorable.

If we are willing to humble ourselves, we can glean much knowledge from countless resources and experts. We must stay curious to keep our dreams alive. We must be willing to stretch and grow in new ways, knowing that there will be growing pains but afterward we will stand stronger and taller. This way, we will be better able to maintain our goal when we reach it.

So let's pack humility, curiosity, and a willingness to stretch and grow.

WE MUST STAY CURIOUS TO KEEP OUR DREAMS ALIVE.

PREPARE SPIRITUALLY AND EMOTIONALLY

There will be many challenges, changes, and joys ahead. That's a guarantee.

For many, trips are stressful. There are fears of not getting to all the places on time, and it is natural for stress to spiral when venturing into the unfamiliar. It can be the same as we journey toward our dreams too. Those feelings can paralyze us, preventing us from reaching for the good God has planned for us.

Spending time in His Word is our best defense. Every day we can read Bible verses that remind us that fear should not hold us back. We can have encouragement all 365 days of the year. The more time we can spend reflecting on what the Bible says, the more we reinforce our faith in the truth. He calls us to be bold and brave.

We have, right at our fingertips, gadgets that can help us search keywords for the struggles we face. Feeling anxious about meeting your first client? Search "Bible verse anxiety." Have stress about how to fund going back to school? Search "Bible verse stress." With each worry we combat with God's message, we enhance our capabilities for success. We stand a little straighter and quiet our hearts. With that strength, we can face clients, scholarship applications, or whatever else initially looms large on our path ahead.

There are many of us who deal with a more constant underlying anxiety and need extra help. Many of the people close to me do. One of the bravest and biggest steps you can take toward fully thriving and enjoying your journey

is getting help from professionals who have more expertise than I can provide as an encouraging friend.

Every single day, I am praying and striving to be better than the day before. The word *striving* often gets a negative spin, since it can identify the type of selfish ambition and empty work toward goals where everything else—including your faith, wellness, and relationships—is neglected. Turning the word into a positive, I see *striving* as using my gifts while working with my faith and those I love to fulfill who I am meant to be. The all-encompassing power in striving to obtain doesn't need to leave us wanting or weary. We can strive by giving our best with balance and awareness of God's direction for us.

For the times when His direction seems to be coming in slowly or getting to the next step in our journey feels a long way off, we need to be sure we've packed a bag full of patience. Trusting His timing may mean leaving our watches behind and letting go of control. This can mean adding healthy expectations for what is to come. We can visualize where we want to be and look at our pretty vision boards while understanding that along the way, things may change—and that doesn't mean we've failed. Our destination just may not look like the picture in our heads.

When we first began looking for a cabin up north, I was looking online all over the Northwoods area. I found a cabin *I knew* was the one. The photos were even on Pinterest and the cover of a magazine. But upon arriving, it was clear the reality did not match the marketed image. The big wrap-around porch wasn't even big enough to put furniture on. There were dust and dead flies everywhere inside the house. The shiny image I had wasn't playing out in real time. But on the drive home, we decided to go a different way and drove through the charming town of Minocqua. I began looking for cabins there, and we found the perfect one for our family.

So let's pack bravery, healthy expectations, patience, and perspective, and let's be open to unexpected detours and surprises that just might lead us to something better than we imagined.

WHAT TO LEAVE BEHIND

When our cabin was still only used as a vacation home, we would trek up there often. The packing became easier and more efficient each time. Maybe the biggest travel hack I employed (thank goodness) was to never leave our city house without cleaning it and having everything picked up. Before our primary home was in the rearview mirror, I made sure it was in a condition I would want to return to a week later. The same practice was used when we left the cabin to go back home.

Keeping that habit of not leaving a mess behind meant that when we arrived at our destination, it was ready to enjoy after the long drive. It was so much more relaxing than pulling in, unloading, and finding work to do right away. I do this now before any of my travels, and I appreciate it every single time.

For our dream journey, we can do the same thing. Let's clear out any old baggage that could weigh us down or make things uncomfortable and start fresh. We can clean up and toss out the debris that came before, including any bad habits, "I can't" phrases, and negative comments we've taken to heart.

Take it from me: Learning these skills will allow you to follow where God is leading you rather than have your journey stalled or stopped by yesterday's junk or other people's stuff. As I've opened my shop and expanded its offerings, I have heard many a "no" along the way. There have been brands I've dreamed of carrying that said no when I first inquired. Though disappointed, I

have grown to trust that something better is up ahead. I have witnessed how the "no" was positive because the timing wasn't right. And I'm learning not to take rejection personally—and that is huge. When we realize not everything that hinders us or doesn't go our way is particularly about us, then we are able to rebound faster and stay on course.

Let's leave behind "I can't," the fear of "no," and the need to take everything personally.

> LET'S CLEAR OUT ANY OLD
> BAGGAGE THAT COULD
> WEIGH US DOWN OR MAKE
> THINGS UNCOMFORTABLE
> AND START FRESH.

SEEING THE SILVER LININGS

During my childhood, my family drove from our home in Texas to the mountains of Colorado for ski trips and summer vacations. I loved these road trips and the memories they built for me. We would stop at the same favorite restaurants, rest stops, and scenic spots each time. My dad would pack the back and top of our SUV with all our bags, our skis, and a cooler full of my mom's frozen casseroles, prepped and ready to enjoy at the condo.

Invariably, some diversion would come along that had the power to disrupt the trip. There were small disappointments, like when the favorite en route Mexican restaurant in New Mexico closed and I couldn't get their honey-drizzled sopaipillas. And there were bigger setbacks, like car troubles that had us stuck in a tiny Texas town for two days, cutting into our time to ski.

If you've had a few disappointing doozies, I bet you can look back on those trips and still notice silver linings. I know I can. Those incidents that were frustrating may now be funny family stories. And the spontaneous situations created by detours can be mined for life wisdom and strength.

When we stay open, when we stay flexible, we can navigate around any disappointments. In our dream journey, this is crucial because disappointments and setbacks will come. If our response to those is practiced, positive, and open, then our rebound is also a sure thing.

We will need to keep a spirit of adventure, trusting that God has a purpose for us even in our struggles. And if we can somehow start to remove or diffuse the negative emotions in these moments, we can appreciate that what we are learning will help us get where we are divinely destined to go and be all the stronger.

Those emotions may be the hardest part to navigate. Keeping with the travel analogy, let's pretend you take the canoe off the top of your car and portage down to the river. As you travel the river, there will be some slow, peaceful spots and some adrenaline-sparking rapids. But there will also be boulders along the edges and a waterfall here or there. Our goal is to paddle steadily, not getting too close to the rocks or near that drop-off. We can approach our emotions the same way: We need to feel them and experience them, but we don't need to let them crash us into the banks or plunge us to rock bottom. Be ready to take time to rest and regain your course and rhythm.

We should also pack humbleness. Being humble will be important along the way. It will help us listen to advice from others. It will help us stay grounded and appreciative of where our blessings come from as we encounter more and more successful moments. Numbers 12:3 says, "Now Moses was a very humble man, more humble than anyone else on the face of the earth." More guidance comes in Micah 6:8: "He has shown you, O mortal, what is good. And what does the Lord require of you? To act justly and to love mercy and to walk humbly with your God."

So let's pack flexibility, openness, humbleness, a sense of adventure…and a great paddle!

FILL UP

We won't get very far if the gas tank is low. It's just as important to fill ourselves with good fuel as it is to fill a vehicle. While we are at it, let's fill ourselves up with the premium kind.

Philippians 4:8 says, "Whatever is true, whatever is honorable, whatever is just, whatever is pure, whatever is lovely, whatever is commendable, if there is any excellence, if there is anything worthy of praise, think about these things" (ESV). That sounds like the kind of fuel I want to be running on. The kind that brings excellence and things worthy of praise.

Where can we find the lovely? The true? The praiseworthy? The joy-sustaining energy? We find this godly fuel when we pay attention to what we are watching, reading, and listening to.

Let's make sure our tank is full. Being self-disciplined and seeking out great resources will help us prepare for and endure our journey. We need to seek out ways to be mentally, emotionally, and spiritually solid to fill up on God's goodness. We need great habits to keep us physically strong and healthy.

JOURNAL THE JOURNEY

- Who are your supporters, mentors, and encouragers, and what about them makes them good company? What type of relationship are you still seeking?

- What else do you need to "pack" for your journey?

- What do you need to fill up with more of? What changes can you make this week toward this?

IN GOOD COMPANY

While we don't put friends in our suitcase, there are people we pack along for our journey. One of the most important things you can do is be intentional about who you surround yourself with as you chase your dream. Your support system has the influence to speak love into you or discourage you.

They say you become the people you spend the most time with. Think for a bit about how you feel around different individuals. My hope is that the main people in your life are encouragers, lifters, and people who help you bloom. Companions who bring out your best are the ones to invite along for the ride.

If you don't have the right kind of people in your close circles, bring some in virtually. You can find inspiring companions or mentors in books and online. Let their wisdom pour into you as you find strength in yourself. As you begin to stretch and meet new people on your journey, you can choose to move toward the people who make you feel good. I'm not talking about people who just tell you what you want to hear; the greatest friends are those who can speak truth into your life in a way that leaves you feeling better, not bruised. The journey toward your dream will be a better one when truth and supportive cotravelers are part of the experience.

So let's buckle up for the ride with the best companions.

Now we are packed and ready. It's time to put the car in drive. So much can be put into the prep and planning that sometimes we can delay the real work that moves us forward. Trust yourself and God's plan; you've prepped and prayed for wisdom and guidance; you've packed what you think you'll need. Let's head toward our great adventure.

BLAZE A TRAIL
MAKE THAT PACKING LIST

Create your packing list so you feel prepared for the journey ahead. What do you want with you to make sure you can not only enjoy but benefit and grow from this adventure?

STARTING DATE:

DREAM:

- [ ] FLEXIBILITY
- [ ] HEALTHY EXPECTATIONS
- [ ] PERSPECTIVE
- [ ] SENSE OF ADVENTURE
- [ ] CURIOSITY
- [ ] HUMOR
- [ ] OPENNESS

- [ ] BRAVERY
- [ ] PATIENCE
- [ ] WILLINGNESS TO GROW
- [ ] BIBLE
- [ ] JOURNAL
- [ ] GREAT COMPANIONS

Add to the list with your personal ideas.

- [ ]
- [ ]
- [ ]
- [ ]

- [ ]
- [ ]
- [ ]
- [ ]

WISDOM ALONG THE WAY

So do not fear, for I am with you;
do not be dismayed, for I am your God.
I will strengthen you and help you;
I will uphold you with my righteous right hand.

ISAIAH 41:10

My times are in your hands;
deliver me from the hands of my enemies,
from those who pursue me.

PSALM 31:15

Being confident of this, that he who began a good work in you
will carry it on to completion until the day of Christ Jesus.

PHILIPPIANS 1:6

NORTHWOODS CONNECTION

On any given day in the Northwoods, you could play car bingo, watching for canoes on top of vehicles, campers being pulled, and bikes on the back racks. This area is a vacation paradise where tourists flock to enjoy a getaway, find peace, and get moving. Summer is full of boating, biking, hiking, and water sports. Winter blesses us with trails for snowmobiling, cross-country skiing, and frozen-lake skating. Packing all the right gear is important; so is knowing where to get it or rent it if you need to. Where can you go to get what you need to get in motion for your season of life? Make a list of resources. Talk to an expert, or pursue classes and information at a local community college, in an online or extension program, or at your town library.

TRY THIS: LUGGAGE TAG

Design a luggage tag. Decorate it with an inspiring verse or quote, a word that motivates, or an image of where you are headed. Attach the tag to your inspiration board or even your backpack so you have the visual in sight to remind you of all the tools, resources, and personal strengths you want to take with you.

6

TRAIL MAP

Your word is a lamp for my feet, a light on my path.

PSALM 119:105

One of the biggest decisions to make as you head out on a journey is figuring out which way to go. Of all the options, which one will be best based on the knowledge and information we have and the advice of the resources available to us?

You may be as old as me and remember having to use paper maps to navigate our way anywhere new. We traveled everywhere like pirates in a movie, unfolding (and trying to refold) our big paper visual of states, towns, and the roads to get there. Then when technology arrived, allowing us to type in our destination and print out the turn-by-turn directions, we couldn't believe the ease it provided.

Now we have a voice that comes from our phone or vehicle telling us each turn to take along the way. Wouldn't it be great to have that for all our decision-making? An easy, clearly communicated indication of which way to go and which step to take as we move forward in life?

TRUST THE PATH MAKER

Thankfully, we do have just that. God is the greatest guide because He sees every obstacle, bump in the road, and victory ahead. God's the Path Maker, and we can trust Him to lead us in the right direction to our flourishing future.

One of the biggest holdups for moving toward that flourishing future is not knowing how to get there. We wonder which path to take and how to know for sure which way God is leading. We may trust that He has the best way marked out, but it's a bit foggy up ahead. How do we get a clear view?

The best way to know the path forward is to consult our compass. The Holy Spirit is our internal instrument. Have you realized it yet? That pulling you feel, like a magnet? It's God's power working through His Spirit in you, pointing you in the right direction. Surrendering to that pull can help us get our bearings and move forward on the route to success.

That pull is revealed as you pray about what's on your heart. Consult the Bible, and see what verses speak to you. Talk to your trusted friends, and when all those arrows point in the same direction, don't delay anymore—step out in faith toward your future.

Sometimes it seems as if there are several ways to go. When I type a destination into my phone's navigation, it makes it clear how to get there and offers up alternative routes for me to consider. One is the fastest, one has the fewest turns, one may avoid highways. The journey our life is on can feel the same way. I don't believe there is only one way to get there. Is it best to go toward our dream in the quickest way possible? Or is it better to take our time? Our Path Maker gives us free will to make choices. We will make mistakes, hopefully learn from them, and get stronger along the way.

> THE BEST WAY TO KNOW
> THE PATH FORWARD IS TO
> CONSULT OUR COMPASS.
> THE HOLY SPIRIT IS OUR
> INTERNAL INSTRUMENT.

FLASHLIGHT OF FAITH

Plotting a course that leaves room for changing direction and space for marvelous moments of spontaneity is the best way to proceed. This preparation and attitude will help us take the journey in stride. As we go, we can navigate along the way as various issues come up. Let's lean into God's wisdom right from the start. We may not know where we are ending up, but God shines a light in front of us to follow when the stretch up ahead is too dark to see.

Some of my favorite memories are summers as a camper and later as a counselor at Pine Cove Camps in East Texas. Flashlights bobbed in the hands of each excited kid making their way through the woods to the campfire at night to sing favorite songs, laugh at skits, and hear messages that could change their life. We didn't expect those little battery-powered flashlights to illuminate the whole forest or even the entire trail. The brightness was just enough for the few footsteps in front of us. But even this much illumination was enough to keep us from stumbling if we were watching the way.

Our flashlight of faith works the same way. God doesn't show us the entire trail ahead—just enough of a view to take the next step. If we had the whole picture, we may never be brave enough to go. At camp, on the way to the firepit, there could be a skunk up ahead that would not want to be noticed or a porcupine that could get a little prickly over the interruption. Along our dream journey, God will clear the way ahead so we have just enough light to see what we can handle right then.

CONTEMPLATION IS THE WAYPOINT

My favorite moments at the lake are when the sun is out and the water has calmed. The trees around the lake are reflected on its glassy surface, and the shifting clouds are mirrored as well and seem to float on the water. It's the kind of view that draws me to go sit on the dock, take in the sight, and reflect on life.

Just as I do on the dock, let's do some personal reflecting now. It's a good time along this journey to stop and observe where we are and where we are headed next on the path, following the arrows God has created for us.

As we pause to reflect on the journey, we may feel excitement, but there may also be some apprehension mixed in. Try to dig deep and identify what you are feeling in this moment. All your feelings are okay. They are valuable. They, along with the compass pull, can provide valuable information. Reflection will help you process your feelings and what they are letting you know. Taking time to reflect when you are not in the deep waters of the big feelings will be most productive.

If you have overwhelming feelings, write about them in your journal. You don't need to write in complete sentences. You don't need to write for anyone other than yourself. Write about them as a prayer. Then when you can take time in a peaceful moment of reflection, pull your journal back out and read through it. Think about what is true in what you are thinking and feeling. Which emotions may be unfounded or arise from an unhealthy viewpoint? If a friend shared these things with you, what advice would you give them? Now say it to yourself.

Feelings can shed light on some precautions and some encouragements, but they shouldn't lead us. Our minds must be in control, choosing which feelings

to let fill our hearts. Choose feelings to help you heal, experience joy, or give you direction, and choose which ones to acknowledge but then move on from.

Taking time for reflection helps us look back and appreciate how strong we are, realize what we have been through in our past, and acknowledge where we are now. Think back and notice how good God is.

Contemplation is the waypoint along the path that lets you rest and stretch. It's not meant to be the destination, but it is a necessary checkpoint. Be careful not to get stuck here, overanalyzing anything. You've probably heard it said that overanalysis leads to paralysis. If we spend too much time thinking about what hasn't gone according to plan, we will miss the unplanned events that have been better than expected. It's a good thing flexibility was one of the things we packed in chapter 5!

If you feel lost in the woods, you've gotten off the trail, or you haven't checked your compass lately, do not lose hope. You have not been alone even for one second.

In the woods of Northern Wisconsin, there used to be active fire towers where rangers would stand watch from way up in the air, looking constantly for smoke and flames. There are only a few of these lookouts left as reminders. My husband, Brian, and I hiked to one recently and we were in awe of the height. We were struck by how dedicated and focused the rangers must have been on their watch from up high. God always has us in His sight from up high too. We may feel like we've lost the trail, but He sees how we are only steps away from getting back on it again.

IF YOU FEEL LOST IN THE WOODS, YOU'VE GOTTEN OFF THE TRAIL, OR YOU HAVEN'T CHECKED YOUR COMPASS LATELY, DO NOT LOSE HOPE. YOU HAVE NOT BEEN ALONE EVEN FOR ONE SECOND.

STAY THE COURSE

My husband and I approach hiking differently. I could hike the same trail over and over, loving the comfort of familiar surroundings and favorite views. Brian wants new adventures and uncharted territory. I'm bold in my own way, but he is less afraid of risk. Though he is still cautious and careful, the challenge of taking on the steepness or extra effort required encourages him to push on. I begin to get more comfortable trying new ways as I get going.

There's a lot to be said for trying new things and pushing our comfort zones. With practice, doing so builds our confidence, and confidence can give us great grounding for the climb. It can be like pulling trekking poles out of our pack. Where before our balance was off and our footing was unsure, the poles give us steadiness. Increased confidence in ourselves found through practicing boldness can keep us steady too.

Another skill we will gain is resilience. As we trip and fall but continue to get back up, we will train our mind and spirit to know that we will be okay. We will be more than okay because we will be stronger.

If you are losing confidence because it is hard for you to see your progress or see God's promises at work in your life, don't lose faith. Stay the course. It will come. Runners talk about that moment when their muscles warm up, their endorphins release, and though their legs have felt like cement, adrenaline spikes and they loosen up and enjoy the run. Keep praying, keep going. If the dream you are pursuing is meant for you, and if you are consistently taking steps toward it, you will get there in God's timing and you will begin to enjoy the journey.

You may also need to lean on others. Let the strength of those mentors and encouragers you've surrounded yourself with come up under you and alongside you to lighten your load.

KEEP ON THE PATH

I thought I'd offer you a few trail markers to pay attention to along the way. These are reminders to stay encouraged, focused, and on track. In each chapter, you can go back and find more assurances in the "Wisdom Along the Way" offerings as well.

Keep an optimistic mindset. Stay positive (Philippians 4:6-7).

Enjoy the journey (Nehemiah 8:10).

You are not alone (Isaiah 43:1-3).

Be strong and courageous (Joshua 1:9).

Do not worry (Matthew 6:34).

Trust the Path Maker (Jeremiah 29:11).

You will make it (2 Corinthians 4:18).

I'm always in awe of how Scripture can comfort and guide, though I shouldn't be. Written so long ago, the words are still perfectly applicable today, and we can take counsel from them forever.

ENJOY THE SCENERY

It is important to me to stay focused and driven but also to be able to slow down and enjoy the process. When we take the blinders off to enjoy the scenery going by, we are reminded of the "why" of the journey and can appreciate the work we are putting into it.

When I get to my shop each day, my to-do list is long. I love checking off each item. I spend a lot of time writing and creating content. As a business owner, there is also a lot of time spent on the daily work of running a company. If I'm not careful, I can miss out on the other part of what I love most about owning a shop—working alongside my amazing staff and interacting with my wonderful customers. The energy I get from being around these groups of great people motivates me for the quiet work in my office. They are the best scenery.

I feel the same way about time with my family. It would be easy to let myself get overwhelmed by the day-to-day running of a busy household. It would be easy to fill my time at home with more

JOURNAL THE JOURNEY

- Is trusting God hard for you? What makes it difficult or easy?

- Which of the "Keep on the Path" reminders speaks to you most where you are on your path right now?

- What are you feeling today on your journey?

writing and work that needs to be done for my business, but I would miss out on so much.

Balance in action would mean finding a way to get where we need to go while also enjoying the scenery. It's talked about so much, especially for and among women. Is it possible? Here's how I think about it: Balance isn't the destination; we don't have to work at getting there just to reach the end. It's a practice we work at each day and try to find joy in.

There are systems I've put into place that really help me save time in my work life and home life so that I have more capacity to enjoy each, therefore keeping my stress lower. Here are a few:

- Do it when I see it. If I see something that needs to be done, I try to do it right away or add it to my to-do list so it's not forgotten.

- Batch tasks for set days. I set one day a week for certain chores— like Tuesdays are when I try to schedule appointments and run errands. Wednesdays, I pay bills, look at the budget, and make any phone calls for maintenance or repairs. And so on.

- Stick to simple routines. In the mornings, I throw in a load of laundry and get the ingredients out to thaw or prep for dinner so they are ready when I get home from work. I try to empty and load the dishwasher so I have a clean sink and counter to come home to.

Taking time to enjoy the scenery lets us fully experience God's presence as He travels beside us the whole way. We can find comfort and reliance through our faith and trust in the one who leads the way. Let's turn on our flashlights to see the path He has cleared just before us—reading, reflecting, and following the trail markers or arrows set for us and enjoying the view along the way.

BLAZE A TRAIL
ESTABLISH A SPECIAL MEMORY BOX

When I was a teacher, I started collecting notes from my students, their parents, and my coworkers in a treasure box of special memories, moments, and appreciations. I did the same when my kids were little, buying underbed boxes to store their favorite school projects, award ribbons, and mementos. Occasionally, just as I do, they pull the boxes out and sort through the memories, amazed to see how they've grown and enjoying the special moments they are reminded of.

Start your own memory box. Use a shoebox or decorate a wooden box from the craft store or an antique cookie tin. Begin to store special souvenirs, notes, and letters to reflect on from time to time. As your stack grows and your box fills, you will also have a visual reminder of the abundance of blessings in your life.

WISDOM ALONG THE WAY

God is within her; she will not fall;
God will help her at break of day.

PSALM 46:5

Be strong and courageous. Do not be afraid or terrified because of them, for
the LORD your God goes with you; he will never leave you nor forsake you.

DEUTERONOMY 31:6

In their hearts humans plan their course,
but the LORD establishes their steps.

PROVERBS 16:9

NORTHWOODS CONNECTION

Life in the Northwoods is full of recreational activities. Many of the adventures on trails require following a map. Often, the same trails we hike during the summer become our cross-country ski trails in the winter. Big maps near the trailhead read "You are Here" and show options of trails to take based on length and difficulty. I like to gather a group to go on ski outings to experience the fun of friendship and also to have extra eyes on the trail directions. Invite some of your friends, and hit a trail near where you live. Make it a regularly occurring activity, taking different paths each time or trying out different locations. If you live in a city, get a walking map of the area or choose a city park to explore as a group. After the adventure, bring home the trail map and frame the memory. If they don't have paper maps, take a photo in front of the sign and frame the print. Start a gallery wall of your hikes, walks, or travels near and far to remind you of the fun and fulfilling feelings of a journey.

TRY THIS: TRAIL MIX

Here are some favorite trail mixes, perfect to bring along on both the road or the path. One of my favorite times to have a trail mix handy was when picking up my kids from school. Somehow having a snack surprise in the car when they jumped in at the end of the day changed complaining about the day into joyful sharing. Making a mix allows you to get creative and choose the best ingredients. They are quick and easy to make ahead, store, and pack for good energy and a special treat.

GORP MIX
raisins
chocolate chips
candy-coated chocolate
peanuts

CHERRY CHIP MIX
dried cherries
chocolate chips
rice cereal
pepitas
cashews

TROPICAL MIX
macadamia nuts
banana chips
dried mango
coconut chips
dried pineapple

S'MORE MIX
Teddy Grahams
mini marshmallows
pretzels
chocolate chips

CHIPMUNK MIX
almonds
walnuts
pumpkin seeds
sunflower seeds
dried cranberries
dark chocolate chunks

FESTIVE MIX
pepitas
dried cranberries
white chocolate raisins
almonds
chocolate chips

BERRY BLAST MIX
dried strawberries
hazelnuts
pretzel sticks
dried blueberries

You can also set out bowls of different ingredients and let everyone mix and make their own.

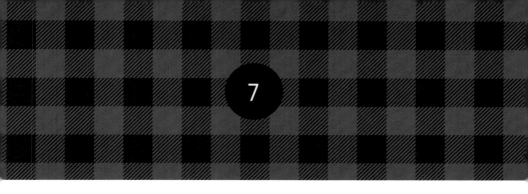

HOPE FOR THE ROAD

And we know that in all things God works for the good of those
who love him, who have been called according to his purpose.

ROMANS 8:28

Following along with the travel and trail language, this chapter is where the rubber meets the road, the boots hit the climb, the tough get going, and the going gets tough.

We've got our dreams in front of us and have set out with great hopes and expectations. But one of the guarantees on our journey is that we are going to run into some roadblocks, come to some forks in the road, and travel down some detours. Though our arrows are pointing the way here and there, as we go, we will bump along some gravel roads and find God's grace.

We need to learn to stay optimistic and hopeful while also being realistic and flexible for the challenges ahead. We need to hold out hope for the road. The best way to do that is to remember that whatever we go through, God will use it for good. We must believe that what is ahead of us is better than what is behind us and do our part to meet Him there—on the path where He guides and directs us along the way.

ROADBLOCKS AND OBSTACLES

Obstacles can appear on the horizon or rise up seemingly out of the blue. Deterrents we anticipate allow us time to prepare, though we still may be scared and apprehensive heading toward them. However, unexpected twists and turns will pop up no matter how ready we are.

Bad habits can stop us in our tracks. Maybe at times we are a little lazy or scroll on social media a bit too long. Just as each of our dreams is unique, so are the patterns that become hindrances to our higher endeavors or even stall our forward momentum. Take some time to identify which habits become roadblocks for you. Once you've identified them, you can plan ways to eliminate them.

Concentrate on one habit at a time so you don't get overwhelmed. The habit you want to change may not be a bad one to fix but rather a new one to implement. For example, years ago, I added an earlier wake-up time to my daily schedule to gain more productive hours. I started by focusing on getting out of bed the moment my alarm went off. Then the rest of my morning routine followed.

Less-than-helpful habits are not the only roadblocks we will face. Naysayers, joy stealers, and critics will also appear, telling us all the reasons our dreams won't work. Don't listen! Hopefully, we have been working on surrounding ourselves with supportive voices, so the negative noise has decreased and cheering has become the loudest sound. Those champions of our dreams may share some cautions with us, but not discouragement. Their wisdom will come in the form of ideas worth thinking through—maybe suggestions altering our course or giving us pause but not advocating an ending.

There may still be critics doling out discouragement, but the biggest critic—our biggest roadblock as we work toward our goals—might simply be ourselves. We can quickly convince ourselves that we are unworthy, unqualified, or not enough.

Let's dispel the myths we make up in our minds and extinguish the excuses we offer up.

One of the fun opportunities that has come along for me is cohosting a podcast with another local business owner. Producing a podcast had been a goal of mine, and during a conversation with my future partner one day, he shared he was working on starting one too. He was further along in developing a plan than I was and had a great concept for a show. I was surprised and grateful when he asked if I'd like to join him.

The decision to join *The Cabincast* didn't take me long to process. I prayed about the decision, and I consulted my husband, a few trusted friends, and my parents before saying yes. There were no discouraging comments from any of them. However, I started to hear some in my own head. Self-talk that shed doubt on how qualified I was, how interesting I would be to listeners, and whether I could provide anything entertaining or enjoyable.

I quickly had to take those thoughts captive before they grew into roadblocks to my dream. In the early days, as I drove to the studio, I would repeat several truths as mantras, reminding myself and reinforcing in my mind and spirit that God had provided me this opportunity and had given me gifts perfectly aligned with this work. Soon, feedback from listeners and growing numbers of those tuning in increased my confidence. But always, even today, I must keep my self-doubting thoughts in check.

Sometimes the roadblocks appear to be more than just barriers, larger than bad habits, and bigger than our own doubts or comments from others. Often, they can seem like unmovable mountains. Luckily, we've got the mover of mountains on the journey with us.

> LET'S DISPEL THE MYTHS
> WE MAKE UP IN OUR MINDS
> AND EXTINGUISH THE
> EXCUSES WE OFFER UP.

GOD MAKES MOUNTAINS MOVE

I taught elementary school for several years after college. Teaching had been my dream for as long as I could remember. As a young girl, more of my time was spent playing school than any other pretend play.

One year, I had a class that was more challenging than usual. Lots of time was spent with my kids working through their conflicts. I was feeling discouraged. Soon after sharing my frustrations with my dad one night over the phone, I received a card in the mail. It was a black-and-white photo of a little girl trying to push a giant boulder. I felt exactly like that little girl. My attempts to get the kids to practice encouragement, positivity, and social skills were coming up against the giant, cold, hard surface of a mountain of negativity. Inside the card was a note from my dad reminding me that I can't move a mountain on my own. It takes faith.

In Matthew 17:20, Jesus says that if we have faith—even as small as a mustard seed—a mountain can move from here to there. There is so much hope and strength in that verse and in the reminder my dad sent to uplift me. That image of not being alone as I face mountains emboldens me to take my little faith and build on it, watching it grow until it is powerful enough to push through the obstacles in front of me. I consistently pray for God to increase my faith.

God's guidance will let us see the mountain moved, or He will give us the arrow to direct us around or over it. We may be meant to climb the peak to learn something through the uphill challenge. God may want us to see the view from the top and look in awe at what we've accomplished.

There are days I feel strong and ready for the climb, and there are others when I'm extremely grateful it only takes a mustard seed.

One day, a few years later, while out running errands, I picked up a blank sketchbook. When I got home, I glued that card inside. Little did I know how that impromptu action would boost my spirits and become part of a roadblock-countering habit. I've continued to add to that sketchbook with phrases, quotes, and cards that remind me of the power of Jesus within me.

FORKS IN THE ROAD

One of the hardest things for me personally is to weed through all the good things—the opportunities, activities, and interests—I have. When all decisions seem good, how can we decide what to do and which way to go? There is only so much time, and we have only so much capacity. If I feel overwhelmed by the decisions I must make, I first try to bring the scenario down to basics and have only two options in front of me at a time.

I've been in the college-mom phase of life now for many years, and I have several more to go. When considering the futures of five kids, the world seems full of so many amazing possibilities. All the great options, though, can become overwhelming and lead to anxiety or even numbness when joy should be the default.

As each one of my kids has made their list of schools, we've worked on paring it down to two choices. Through online research, campus tours, or even conversations with current students or professors, some schools were quickly removed from the list, while others remained possibilities. Bringing the shrinking list down to two greatly helped our conversations be based on logic and some feelings. The logic factors—majors, amenities, location, financial aid—all

matter, but feelings do too. How did they feel on campus? How did they feel when talking to people from the school?

In my own college-visiting experience, I felt at home instantly on one campus where students walking by me consistently smiled and said hello. There wasn't another campus where I had that same experience. And that feeling stuck, as I had four marvelous years at Coe College in Cedar Rapids, Iowa.

This strategy of paring down the options can work as you look at possibilities for choosing a new job, moving to a different town, going back to school, or learning to play an instrument or speak a new language. Bring all the amazing choices down to two instead of many. Then look at it logically *and* with attention to your feelings.

I've found this to be helpful in situations where I can bring the decision-making down to the simplest two options of *yes* or *no*. When you are asked to commit to something, to attend an event, or even to eat another helping of pasta, keep it simple. Decide *yes* or *no* rather than muddling your mind and the circumstance with a bunch of *what-ifs* or emotions (guilt, anyone?) running through your head.

Always remember that *yes* and *no* are complete answers. You don't need to offer explanations or justifications for your decisions.

JOURNAL THE JOURNEY

- Are you waiting for a miracle? Write a prayer about what's on your heart.

- What is your current "fork-in-the-road" experience? Spend time imagining you took the first road. Now follow the other road with your imagination. Journal about how each feels and which choice sits right in your spirit, heart, and mind.

- Write a reflection about a mountain you've come up against and how you got over or around it. What did you learn from that experience that can help you the next time you encounter one?

DETOURS AND DIRT ROADS

Songs and poems are written about how detours that seemed disastrous at the time lead you to exactly where you were supposed to end up. When a detour comes, give yourself permission to feel frustrated and maybe a bit sad for a short amount of time, and then move on. That is the key to not letting detours derail us—moving on and following the detour to see where it goes.

As each experience ends or changes, it deserves the moments and feelings that let it become a memory (good or bad) to shape and strengthen us in preparation for what's next. But we can't stay stuck trying to continue where there is no road ahead. We must continue in a new way, on a path that is altered a bit or a great deal. Each detour, taken with bravery, will build our resilience. The new secondary way may require us to learn something new, develop a new skill, or leave something behind.

About a year after opening my shop, it became obvious that we needed more space for our growing inventory and our many ideas for new programming and events. A location was available that seemed like the perfect fit. We met with the realtor, took tours, put in our offer, and had it accepted. We began meeting with contractors to plan a few exciting changes to make the space our own.

Then we got a call. There was a zoning issue with an adjacent business that couldn't be easily resolved. I felt discouraged. I felt sad that what I had envisioned wouldn't become a reality. But separate from my feelings, I knew that this must mean God had a better location in mind. So I took the new path and kept my eyes open for another opportunity. He brought it to me when a realtor called to ask if we were interested in a spot that was about to go on the market. We said yes, and after going through the process again—this time with no diversions—we moved the shop to its new home, which feels perfectly meant to be.

Sometimes we might want to take one of the side paths presented. Instead of a forced detour, we may decide to take the dirt path that few have pursued rather than the paved one with many travelers going at faster speeds. It may take us a little longer to get to our dream destination when we do, but we could very well be richer for the experience. There's adventure there, usually great scenery, and a chance for a possibility we haven't predicted.

EACH DETOUR, TAKEN WITH BRAVERY, WILL BUILD OUR RESILIENCE.

GRAVEL ROADS AND GRACE

It will get bumpy up ahead no matter which way we go. What's your favorite way to travel? Several years ago, I lost the enjoyment for air travel I'd had since I was a kid. I still fly—it's often necessary on family trips or for work—but I'd always rather drive. What I like least about flying is the turbulence. It comes down to the loss of control I feel over the bumps. I fully acknowledge that it's an unfounded fear I only apply to myself. I don't have a fear of my loved ones flying, but for some reason, when it gets rough up above, I quietly struggle.

One day out on the lake, cutting across the waves in our boat, I started thinking about how it was bumpier on the lake than it has ever been in the air (that I have felt). This made me pay attention to some of the drives I had where the roads were bumpy too.

The bumps I feel are relative. It depends on where I'm at and how I'm traveling.

I've found my favorite comfort for those bumpy times on a flight. I could tell myself that it's just like riding across the lake in our boat, but that hasn't worked yet. What has helped is to watch the flight attendants and notice how calm they are. As they stay relaxed and smiley, even continuing with the drink service while I'm buckled up, my confidence grows and so does my peace.

When our dream journey gets bumpy, we can look for the same support by traveling with others who either have taken the path before or are headed the same way. Join a club, a support group, or a class. If there's not one near you, there's probably a virtual one. Be bold and start your own, reaching out to others you know would be helpful in keeping you motivated. Maybe everyone in the group isn't aiming for the same goal, but they are all dream-chasers willing to keep one another accountable. Find a prayer partner who will keep you lifted as you go and will calmly call upon Jesus when you feel the bumps, reminding you to look to Him for your peace.

Thank goodness for God's grace when we make mistakes, take wrong turns, or embark on the detour armed with faith alone. His grace is a guarantee that overshadows all the missteps behind us and illuminates all the turns and curves ahead. With Him, we get a chance to get back on track.

BLAZE A TRAIL

KEEP A NOTEBOOK OF PROMISES

In your journal, keep track of any roadblocks, detours, and bumps in the road you encounter. Place each on a separate page with the date. Occasionally, go back and look over them. Add to those pages what you learned from those challenges, what is still hard because of them, or the blessings you see because of what you avoided or boldly pushed through.

In this same notebook, consider creating a source of encouragement like I did years ago with that sketchbook and the card from my dad. Write down verses or quotes that speak to your journey. Include cards and notes and other reminders that you are not alone along the way. You will build your own pathway of promises that will get you through the tough times.

WISDOM ALONG THE WAY

Consider it pure joy, my brothers and sisters, whenever you face trials of many kinds, because you know that the testing of your faith produces perseverance. Let perseverance finish its work so that you may be mature and complete, not lacking anything.

JAMES 1:2–4

Not only so, but we also glory in our sufferings, because we know that suffering produces perseverance; perseverance, character; and character, hope. And hope does not put us to shame, because God's love has been poured out into our hearts through the Holy Spirit, who has been given to us.

ROMANS 5:3–5

I know what it is to be in need, and I know what it is to have plenty. I have learned the secret of being content in any and every situation, whether well fed or hungry, whether living in plenty or in want. I can do all this through him who gives me strength.

PHILIPPIANS 4:12–13

NORTHWOODS CONNECTION

I've lived in big towns, I've lived in small towns, and I've visited both. I must admit, I've completely become a small-town girl after living in the Northwoods of Wisconsin. This tourist area grows seasonally, especially in the summer. I think one of the things tourists love even more than the beautiful lakes, recreational activities, water ski shows, and supper clubs is getting to be part of our small-town experience. This small-town feeling can be found anywhere, though, even if you live somewhere with a big population. In your neighborhood, at your work, at your kids' school, these aspects of small-town life can become the norm.

Be welcoming and friendly. Be excited to run into a familiar face. Stop to chat awhile. Shop at and support local small businesses and fundraisers.

TRY THIS: COLLECT AND SEND CARDS

Start collecting cards when you see special ones, pretty ones, or inspiring ones in gift shops or even dollar stores. Keep them in a box with a pen and some stamps. Add to your good habits the practice of writing a card out each day to encourage, thank, or celebrate someone. Drop it in the mail, on their desk at work, or at their front door. Something amazing will start to happen. You'll encourage your own heart as you remind others that they aren't alone. Taking only a few minutes out of your day can make a lasting impact, just like with the card my dad sent me.

8

PADDLE YOUR OWN CANOE

Therefore encourage one another and build each other up.

1 THESSALONIANS 5:11

When I was in high school, I was on the newspaper staff, eventually becoming editor my senior year. Writing about campus news was all about the *who, what, where, when,* and *why.* We could write informative stories about what happened and when and where it took place, but the biggest question was always the *who*—who was involved? That's what made the story engaging, relevant, and personal.

The *who* matters.

And in the dream journey, the *who* matters too. You are the traveler on this trek, the *who* on your unique adventure. There's a phrase a lot of us have heard as a life analogy, and I've certainly also heard it as a lake-town resident: "Paddle your own canoe." It traditionally means to be independent and self-reliant. But my definition of it is so much bigger and better for our pursuit of purpose. To me, paddling our own canoes means that we are to live our lives according to our unique gifts and callings. God is our guide pointing us in the right direction, but we have the paddles in our hands and need to carve the way in the water.

This version leads us to fulfillment in *our* flourishing life and leaves us with zero time or desire to criticize or worry about others. In fact, it inspires us to ask others to come along with us, each paddling in our own style and toward our own destination.

This slight reframing of the adage reminds us that cheering on others or benefiting from the encouragement and instruction of another is a good thing because, while we may be paddling uniquely and for different reasons, we are ultimately all on the water together.

Our friends, family, supporters, and mentors make a difference. The people we keep around us as encouragers, those we meet through chance encounters, and even the authors and speakers we pay attention to help us on our course and make the paddling worth it.

GOD IS OUR GUIDE POINTING US IN THE RIGHT DIRECTION, BUT WE HAVE THE PADDLES IN OUR HANDS AND NEED TO CARVE THE WAY IN THE WATER.

CAN'T DO ALL THE THINGS

I'm a want-to-do-all-the-things girl. I want to accept the invitation to dinner out with the girls and, at the same time, be home for the evening with my family. I want to work full time in my shop, be home creating content and putzing around my house, get my masters, and speak at women's conferences. Whew! See? All the things. I'm an idea person interested in much, and I'm also content in so many places and situations.

Are you the same way, or are you someone who functions on the other end of the spectrum? Maybe you need to give yourself a little push to get out there and try something new or be out and about in new arenas. Or maybe it is hard for you to find your way to contentment.

No matter how we personally paddle our canoes, we need to understand our approach to life and our capacity for growth. The right answers for you and the right answers for me are found when we are involved in but not consumed by our pursuits and interests.

In Exodus, when Moses encountered a burning bush, what caught his eye and aroused his curiosity was that the bush was not being destroyed by the flames. A burning bush in the desert would probably not have been remarkable, but this one was miraculous because, while it kept burning, it also remained whole and alive. It wasn't devoured, drained, depleted, devastated, or demolished. Are the things you're paddling toward consuming you? Leaving you feeling devoured, drained, depleted, and so on? If so, that's not where God wants you.

You'll know you are in the right place and doing the right-for-you activities when you thrive instead of feeling used up and burned out.

COMPARISON SINKS YOUR CANOE

A gift of paddling our own canoe is that we're moving at our own pace. And a hard aspect of paddling our canoe is also that we're moving at our own pace. We will occasionally see friends or strangers cruising by us at enviable speeds. We will watch people reach their goals more quickly. It will happen. And because we're human, we'll occasionally be frustrated by this. We need to just keep going forward and not let the winds and waves coming our way cause us to adjust our position.

One of the biggest gusts that can set a person off their course is the powerful force known as social media. With one scroll, we can be swayed and rocked by random shiny things, falsehoods, and even good things other people are doing that distract us from our own good things.

Spending time each day on social media is part of my job. I create and share content to encourage others, exhibit my craft (writing, decorating, hospitality), and bring more customers to my shop. But I must be careful. Social media can suck us down rabbit holes that steal our time, positivity, and productiveness. It can give us unrealistic expectations and the tendency to compare and feel "less than."

There are a lot of things on social media that can make my heart hurt. Things that can make me sad, frustrated, and crabby. There are also things that can make me feel like I'm not enough, I don't have enough, I'm not pretty enough, I'm not far enough along my journey. The *enoughs* can go on and on, so I tell myself, "That's enough of feeling that way!"

I remind myself that I am enough, remembering who God says I am: "For we are God's handiwork, created in Christ Jesus to do good works, which God prepared in advance for us to do" (Ephesians 2:10).

If I feel inklings of comparison or jealousy, I turn those feelings around by thinking kind thoughts. For example, instead of thinking, "I wish I had a kitchen that nice." I think, "They did such a beautiful job on their kitchen." Instead of thinking, "Why did she get that opportunity?" I think, "She deserves this!"

The shift from comparison to kindness will encourage you on your own journey because it will transform your thoughts, including your self-talk. It's so much lighter and more enjoyable to see the good in a situation, in others, and in yourself.

PROTECTING OUR HEAD AND HEART SPACE

I have found social media platforms full of inspiration, teaching, and encouragement because that's what I'm choosing to focus on while scrolling past what is negative, belittling, or discouraging.

When we look for them, we can find and form amazing friendships with women around the world who share similar interests. I've heard uplifting talks, sermons, and lessons from renowned teachers. I've gathered ideas for wonderful new recipes, workout plans, and fixes and hacks for dozens of dilemmas. However, even with all this good, I must be careful. I must set some boundaries for myself and guard what matters. To protect our heart space, we must guard our headspace.

One bit of wisdom for protecting my headspace came from a mentor group I was in with Liz Marie Galvan and her husband Jose. Liz Marie shared, "Create more than take." That phrase comes to mind often as I try to set time limits for what I'm watching or listening to. There truly is so much good out there, but God has things He wants me to do and create. So I set limits for how long and how much I take in. I practice self-discipline so there is plenty of time and opportunity for me to create, share, and put good out into the world in whatever way God is leading me. To honor where my canoe is headed, I want to use my voice, presence, and any platform to uplift and serve and represent what I value.

To walk the talk, I must also be attentive to what I value in real time and in real life. This means being intentional about putting my phone down so I can fully focus on the moment and the people God has brought into my life. A few safeguards that have helped me are the following:

- staying off social media on the weekends
- leaving my phone charging in the bathroom at night instead of on my nightstand
- setting timers when I jump on an app that might suck me in

Social media, like any other resource, is a tool, and we're in charge of how we use it. Understanding our purpose for being on any of the outlets helps us maintain boundaries and a healthy perspective. This may require us to ask ourselves why we're spending time on each of the platforms and using our answer to set parameters on how much time we will spend each day or week on them (if at all), which platforms serve or support our paths, what types of content we will watch, what forms of content we will create or highlight, and who we will follow.

How about a little recap?

Remember to "create more than take."

Understand your "why."

Set time limits.

Decide which platforms fit the way you enjoy receiving content.

Use your voice to honor and lift up what matters to you.

TO PROTECT OUR HEART SPACE, WE MUST GUARD OUR HEADSPACE.

FOCUS ON WHAT'S TRUE, WHAT MATTERS

A lot of heartache and discouragement can be avoided if we focus on what is true rather than what our minds misconstrue as fact. I see this played out in relationships often, especially when communication comes from not a live conversation but a digital one. There can be misinterpretations and misunderstandings that lead to hard feelings and even ill-fated decisions or changes of plans.

In all situations, rather than creating your own version of what someone meant by what they said (or wrote), or assuming someone is ignoring you, or supposing they don't like you or that they are misleading you, stop and ask yourself what you know to be true. If you can't answer that, then presume the best instead of the worst. Usually, the better version will be the most accurate.

Often, other people aren't thinking about us at all, anyway. They are too busy thinking about themselves or the destination ahead of them.

Sometimes a truth we discover is that we need to set boundaries with a family member or friend. They are people we care about, yet we know their influence on our life is potentially unhealthy. As hard as it may be, setting boundaries so that you don't have roller-coaster relationships, negative energy, or emotionally draining dialogues is vital to your own health and happiness. The good news is that we don't have to build walls, but we do need to add hedges and limit the amount of time these people have in our presence, whether that's in person, on the phone, or online.

RISING TIDES

The lake we live on is surrounded by homes—some are lived in full time, some are used seasonally, and some are vacation rentals. There's a historic resort across the bay from our cabin with over 20 charming white cottages with green trim. It fills weekly with employees from a big company and their families—a fun perk of their jobs.

Many other lakes in the area, like ours, have ways for residents and visitors to gather and enjoy the water together. There are groups who are interested in learning more about and protecting the loons. There are book clubs, sunrise

JOURNAL THE JOURNEY

- Currently, do you feel you are taking more or creating more? How do you feel about that?

- Have you had a misunderstanding with someone? Write about it, and then reread what you wrote. Does it change how you view the situation?

- In what areas of your life do you compare yourself to others?

yoga clubs, and paddle clubs. For example, the paddle clubs designate a time and place, and everyone brings their kayak, canoe, or SUP (stand-up paddle-board) to get a workout in beautiful surroundings while making friends.

The encouragement we get from others needs to go both ways. We are not just sponges and takers. We have a lot to give as well and will be more enriched for the giving. I believe, as John F. Kennedy said, "Rising tides lift all boats." When people come together for a common purpose, whether it's to learn something, have a fun time, or take on an important cause, everyone is built up and each person's potential is elevated.

Some of the richest relationships in my life are with the women I work with at my shop, White Arrows Home. As the staff was brought together, it was important to me to find ladies who were going to be not just employees but amazing, talented workers who loved to dream big too. Positive ladies who are self-motivated and tons of fun were the perfect fit.

I believe that we work best by encouraging one another in our endeavors at the shop and outside it as well. Letting everyone "do their thing" while we all jump in to help as needed lets everyone's talents shine. We all listen to one another's ideas, talk through the challenges that come up, and focus on the customer experience and work environment we create. Daily, we talk through our "wins" to keep our focus on the good. One of our mottos is that we are "so much more than home decor."

Our relationships can be so much more when we lift up others. Just as the rising tide lifts every boat, we can be the supporter who helps those around us rise and paddle forward with assurance and hope.

LEARN FROM OTHERS

We can learn a great deal from those around us. Sometimes the knowledge and info may not even come from a positive situation. We can learn from disappointments like bad bosses and frustrated customers too. A perspective shift

may be needed to see the negative experience or encounter as a path to growth. Those situations or people teach us how *not* to act, handle conflicts, or lead.

Search out speakers, podcasters, and authors you can learn from or be inspired by. There are so many inexpensive or even free ways to gain more understanding. Schedule time in your day to listen and read. Use your driving time, chore time, or waiting time to learn. I love to take some downtime to scroll through my favorite apps and social media, but I use those time limits so I then have more time to start the audiobook that's been on my list.

Be gracious to others who offer help and advice as those around you become excited about your journey. As we become surrounded by those who believe in us, we will enjoy the adventure and grow more. It will help us find strength on the way to encourage others in their goals too.

We may be solo in our canoe, but we're never alone on the water. There are others around doing their best to paddle their way forward too. As they come alongside us, we will remember not to compare, to set boundaries if needed, and to embrace the encouragers. We will also remember we have the greatest friend along too, one who actually walks on water: Jesus.

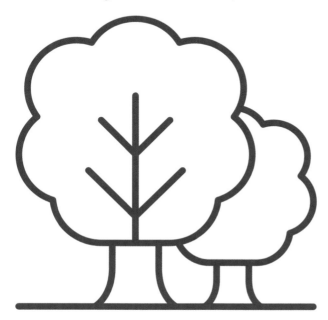

BLAZE A TRAIL
BUILD YOUR PERSONAL LIBRARY

Curate a library of books that inspire you. Start reading books that teach you more about your business, hobbies, or healthy habits. Use highlighters, sticky notes, or pencils to mark parts that you want to remember. Collect the books on a bookshelf where they can be visual reminders and referenced as needed. Be ready to share the titles with others when you think they can be helpful. Make a stop often to add one of them to a local Little Free Library and spread the encouragement. Maybe build your own Little Free Library for your yard, your kids' school, or your neighborhood where you can add books once in a while for others to learn from too.

WISDOM ALONG THE WAY

Do not be misled: "Bad company corrupts good character."

1 CORINTHIANS 15:33

Two are better than one,
because they have a good return for their labor.

ECCLESIASTES 4:9

Be devoted to one another in love. Honor one another above yourselves.

ROMANS 12:10

NORTHWOODS CONNECTION

After living in the Northwoods of Wisconsin for a couple months, we were amazed at the many opportunities to see unique and breathtaking moments in nature. We often spot eagles soaring across the sky. And it's possible that just on the way to the grocery store, I will see a fox dash out of the pines, or I will have to slow down to let a mama black bear and her cubs cross the road. The loons sing lullabies on summer nights.

God wants us to take part in all the beauty He provides. Keep your eyes open for those beautiful reminders throughout your day. It may be as simple as finding a heart-shaped rock on a walk. My mom has a collection of heart rocks in her garden that were found on her travels and received as gifts from her grandkids.

Is there something that always catches your eye? Maybe a cardinal or shapes in the clouds? As soon as we start to pay attention, we will see those beautiful visuals reminding us of God's presence and love.

TRY THIS: BEAUTIFUL REMINDERS

If something stands out to you, find a special way to display and remember it. Frame a leaf, press flowers, keep a basket of shells, start a collection. When you see an animal you don't know much about, do some research and learn more. Think of this new knowledge as a reminder of how nature shows God's love for you and a promise of His power to continue in you—His masterpiece.

SNOW DAY

Come to me, all you who are weary and burdened, and I will give you rest.

MATTHEW 11:28

How do you live up there in winter?" I'm asked this question often by people who assume the long duration of our winters, sometimes spent under a blanket of 100 inches of snow, makes life too hard, unbearable even. They think the temperatures that drop below zero will freeze out the joy. But the truth is, I love living in the Northwoods in every season—even winter.

When the flakes accumulate into large formations, we still get out and stay active; we just dress for the weather. Snowshoeing, cross-country skiing, snowmobiling, and ice-skating keep us active and busy. Though the activities are fun, my favorite parts of winter are the cozy moments spent by the roaring fireplace and the excuse to slow down and hibernate a bit.

Contentment and gratitude come down to a state of mind—no matter which geographic state you live in. Whether you live in frozen northern regions or places where winter means simply a shift toward chillier evenings, winter reminds us to take unhurried moments and experience rest and restoration in big ways.

Every now and then, one of my favorite announcements arrives by phone or a news break: School is canceled! The schools are calling for a snow day. The blank-slate day this provides is a gift. Can it be inconvenient sometimes? Absolutely. Is it the permission we didn't realize we were waiting for to rest, play, and restore? Absolutely.

A snow-day mindset invites us to embrace where we are and see the good. In the life season you are in, this can be the reboot you need, the reminder to take time for yourself all year long. Implementing cozy practices and habits will refill you mentally, physically, and spiritually and build the strength and stamina you need to chase dreams every day.

SELF-CARE, SMALL CHANGES

When I'm depleted, tired, exhausted, or stressed, I'm not able to move the needle far. I can become paralyzed and unable to make any forward motion or gain the focus and energy necessary to be productive. I've found strategies that start with basic steps of self-care to regain momentum and a positive attitude. These practices don't take much time or effort, yet it's surprising how hard it is to do the little things that make us feel better. But if we commit to beginning, if we simply set out each morning to add in a few good practices, layering them as we go, we will form a routine that's good for our body and soul.

Even small changes matter and have a big impact.

One of the smallest shifts you can make is a physical one. First, be conscious of your posture. Do you end up curled over a phone, tablet, or computer either scrolling, reading, or working? Spend a day keeping track of how often you end up in a hunched position. When I finally paid attention, I was shocked by my frequent bad posture. That day, I started to take more pauses to stand and walk.

To break out of the bad-posture pose and into a new habit, roll your shoulders back, look up, then look forward. You will be amazed how the act of straightening up can give your confidence and energy levels a boost. When

you walk around, try turning your hands so that your thumbs face forward—this will give your shoulders and back good alignment.

You may be like me and spend a good deal of time typing and reading, so add reminder notifications in your phone to stand and stretch frequently enough that you feel more blood flow, a release in your back, shoulders, and hips. You will notice an improvement in energy levels.

Daily workouts really help me too. Do you have an activity you love to do? Are you able to be motivated on your own, or do you need a trainer or group class? Everyone is different. I find that when I am in a good fitness routine, I feel so much happier and more productive. I feel my confidence increase. I feel my mood elevate. When I'm not in a good routine, I experience the opposite; I feel like I'm barely treading water. It's amazing how quickly being out of routine can bring me down and how hard it is to start back up. But once I start (that's the key—starting), all the good feelings rush back.

A few things that have helped me may also help you start or keep your workouts a priority. We have a home gym, which you would think would make workouts easy to accomplish. It does help, but it still takes self-discipline to get there. In the morning, I must tell myself to get dressed, make my way to the workout area, and do something. Anything. Even if it's just a short spin on the bike, a slow walk on the treadmill, a few swings of the kettlebell. It never fails that my "do a little" turns into "do a little more."

When something is visible, it's harder to ignore. So I set my workout clothes and running shoes where I can see them. And I have motivational quotes and inspirational photos in my line of sight to give me a boost.

IMPLEMENTING COZY
PRACTICES AND HABITS
WILL REFILL YOU
MENTALLY, PHYSICALLY,
AND SPIRITUALLY AND
BUILD THE STRENGTH
AND STAMINA YOU
NEED TO CHASE
DREAMS EVERY DAY.

Do rewards incentivize you? Set goals where you honor your effort with some perks. Maybe after two weeks of consistent workouts, you splurge on a pedicure. Maybe after six weeks, a new pair of running shoes. Soon, the good feeling of being consistent will be enough.

I love plants and flowers, but I'm not a natural plant caregiver. It's something I work at. My thumbs are not green. But I've learned that seeing live plants and deep greens calms me. The time I take to water and tend to them that helps them thrive also helps me slow down and find space for peace. Adding some fresh herbs to my recipes or mint to my water is a quick, easy way to signal to myself that I matter. In the winter, when herbs aren't growing in my raised bed, I keep them in mason jars in the fridge.

Bringing home an inexpensive bouquet of grocery store flowers gives me

a lift. I love looking around in my home for one of my vintage containers (a thermos, jug, can, or vase) to style the flowers in, then setting it on the kitchen island or my nightstand to enjoy for several days.

Along with surrounding myself with fresh plants, flowers, and herbs, shopping for fresh fruits and vegetables nourishes me deeply. I try to implement some meal prepping into my week to save time and slow down and appreciate what I'm putting into my body. The beautiful colors of sliced sweet potatoes, avocados, strawberries, and so on are a rainbow reminder of God's love for me.

The blessing of choosing whole foods and being intentional as we prepare and enjoy them is that the physical and mental nourishment we receive is far deeper than if we had grabbed quick, nonnutritious snacks. And since we're eating healthy, let's not forget to hydrate well. (Enjoy a favorite water refresher from chapter 4!)

As we take care of our own needs, we become fortified and able to then serve and bless others while having enough extra energy to keep moving toward our dreams.

MAKE ROOM FOR NEW HABITS

While we are building new habits, trying something new, or making a move, everyday life is still going on. It is easy to get overwhelmed by what is expected, required, or demanded of us, and when we add new goals to our lists, life can really get overwhelming. But don't worry. When you embrace your thought-out goals, you head toward habits that will eventually ease the overwhelm and allow for an enduring peace.

One of the things that helps me is to remember that there are seasons for everything. As I get busier with one aspect of a change or new challenge, I will need to cut myself some slack and give myself some grace in another.

We're most overwhelmed when we feel we're going under. If we're drowning in our to-dos and tempted to second-guess our dreams, then all we may need is to tweak our daily schedule and loosen up our personal expectations. Revisiting our list of demands and desired objectives and examining where our time is going will help us decide what to reduce or rein in.

The decisions aren't always easy, but putting some limits in place and prioritizing what we spend time on will serve us well. In the last year, I have tried to schedule all my appointments and errands on Tuesdays. This has helped me focus on work the other days of the week rather than have interrupted schedules. Similarly, I try to only add two evening social activities a month that take me away from my family.

Look at your last month's schedule. Have you felt too busy? Are there some limits you could set for yourself? What's a comfortable decision for you in this season? When declining or canceling commitments, remember you don't need to give excuses and explanations. A kind response of "This week won't work; I hope to join in another time soon" or simply "I'm not adding anything to my schedule this month" is enough. Usually, the fewer words, the better.

JOURNAL THE JOURNEY

- Is there a way prayer, care, movement, or revised expectations could turn some moment in your day into a time that resets your heart and mind?

- Describe what a day of restoration could look like. How does it make you feel to anticipate such a day? Set a date on your calendar!

- What small act of self-care can you add to your day? How would it help you?

RESET WHEN STRETCHED THIN

I've shared that it's easy for me to want to jump in and do it all. My capacity is vast, but there's not enough room or resources to do everything. I end up doing a lot well instead of a few things great. When I start feeling stretched too thin, I notice I have less patience. Instead of feeling like the juggler, keeping all the balls in the air, I feel like one of the balls, trying to find a rhythm. My usual enthusiasm and energy wane, and I start craving more sleep than I know I need.

Like the computers and phones we utilize daily, sometimes we need a simple reset to function better.

Returning to simple measures and self-care practices can go a long way toward recentering ourselves. Rather than feeling stretched thin, we can take some time to stretch out. A simple five-minute stretching session with some deep breathing can restore your shape, so to speak. It can draw the extended parts of yourself back in so you feel whole. Download an exercise app, or search for online stretch routines to make this an accessible activity.

A quick reset can happen by getting in motion. The self-care practices from earlier—especially the movement and nourishment—will initiate a reset. And sometimes I reset by doing something more settled and grounded. My daughters and I started home spa nights on Sunday evenings. We do face masks and paint our nails and toes while watching a movie together. It gives us a great, consistent time together that we look forward to and helps us celebrate the end of a week and kick off a new one in a fun way.

Resetting our hearts and the focus of our minds is a way to breathe peace into our routines and lives. Winter is very dark up north, and a person can start to dread the long nights. So to reset my attitude and spirit, I found a way to bring light into the darkness. Each evening at dusk, I turn off the overhead lights and walk around the house turning on the lamps. As I do, I pray through the rooms, thanking God for the blessing of this shelter from the elements and asking His guidance for what is on my mind at the time.

Then I pour a warm drink into a favorite mug and curl up in my favorite chair by the fire. Whether chatting with my husband and kids, reading, or working awhile, the comfort of being cuddled up settles me inside and out. I've come to crave the lamplit nights.

Think about your least favorite part of your regular schedule or the point in the day when you hold a bit of resistance. How can you bring light into the situation?

> RESETTING OUR HEARTS AND THE FOCUS OF OUR MINDS IS A WAY TO BREATHE PEACE INTO OUR ROUTINES AND LIVES.

RESTORE AND EXPLORE

One of the most popular product lines in my shop is our collection of restored clothing. My team and I carefully choose and curate clothes from our favorite brands that have been worn before and are still in mint condition. We hope to keep more textiles out of landfills. We find joy in knowing these classy clothes will have new life and help our customers make amazing memories while feeling beautiful.

This is the same way we can restore ourselves too. Like these items of clothing, we want to continue to be useful, and we can do that by being refreshed, rejuvenated, and restored.

Have you been feeling as though your age is catching up to you? Are there days when you wonder if you

are unworthy of your deep wishes? Do you let the memories of your mistakes cloud your chances for success?

It does not matter how old we are. It does not matter what our insecurities, doubts, or past failures have taken from us. What matters is knowing we have a good, great God of miracles who specializes in restorations. God requires our trust and patience for the process and a willingness to meet Him right where we're at, even if it feels hard or messy. He will be there and bring us out the other side stronger and better.

This side of heaven, we can find restoration in rejuvenating practices. Some of my favorite ways to find rejuvenation start on either end of the action spectrum. I might discover restoration by becoming quiet in prayer or gazing at the water. Or I might feel restored and reinvigorated by getting busy, exploring, stepping out in wonder, and embracing nature. I like experiencing both—I need them both. Some practices combine the two. If I go for a walk, the movement and the meditative aspect restore my energy. I highly recommend that you take off your shoes and walk in the grass, feeling the ground under your feet, to still and revitalize your spirit. My chance to fill up comes when I find balance between being a homebody and being social while learning to listen to what my needs are.

Finding our just-right balance requires a certain amount of listening to yourself. If you had a perfect week, how much of it would be spent with others, and how much would be spent in homebody mode? Notice these things so you grow in your understanding of how you can change for the better, learn new things, and find a fresh start.

Speaking of fresh starts, I believe that to experience restoration, we must find forgiveness, give forgiveness, and forgive ourselves. So much energy can be wasted on feelings of guilt or blame. When we tend to our past hurts and bring them to light for healing (rather than bury them under a rock), we are freed to follow God's arrows with much less baggage weighing us down.

YOUR SEASON TO "BEAR"

It's okay to rest, to put your feet up, to lounge around. I am not a napper; when I lie down, all I do is think about what else I could be doing. But still there are ways I can kick back and take a break. Are you refreshed after a quick nap? If you had a chunk of time and no agenda, if the to-do list could wait, if you were just staying home, how would you spend it?

Is there a way to schedule days of "no schedule" into your life? Could you truly rest one Saturday a month or on Sundays? There are times when it is wise to be like the black bears that roam our area. They know when it is the right season to hibernate. When we commit to seasons of rest, it lets us come out into our spring, into the next season—or even the following Monday—ready to get going with passion, enthusiasm, and a refreshed spirit.

We may not be able to disappear into a den in the woods for months, but we can adopt a rhythm of restoration. Let's embrace the season we are in and find ways to grow in it with a balance of work and rest.

BLAZE A TRAIL
PLAN A PERSONAL RETREAT

Set up your own personal retreat either in your home or at a favorite weekend getaway. Leave behind any pressing work and your taskmaster mindset, and bring with you only activities, projects, or inspirations that you find relaxing.

Let yourself linger, stroll, savor. Try keeping your phone in a separate space from you. Don't worry about the time—just take your time. Read, do a craft project, or spend a couple hours daydreaming like you did as a kid. Become lost in thought or what you are doing, and enjoy the uninterrupted moments. If napping is your treat, then snuggle up and snooze.

WISDOM ALONG THE WAY

In peace I will lie down and sleep, for you alone,
LORD, make me dwell in safety.

PSALM 4:8

There remains, then, a Sabbath-rest for the people of God; for anyone who
enters God's rest also rests from their works, just as God did from his.

HEBREWS 4:9–10

Take my yoke upon you and learn from me, for I am
gentle and humble in heart, and you will find rest for your
souls. For my yoke is easy and my burden is light.

MATTHEW 11:29–30

✖ NORTHWOODS CONNECTION

Winter in the Northwoods is wonderful. When fresh snow (which comes often) falls and flocks the trees, it's as beautiful as a movie set. Taking time to build a fire in the fireplace brings so much satisfaction, especially after just coming in from the cold and hanging up our coats or flannels. Everywhere in this region, you see people bundled in plaid wool jackets, hats, and flannel shirts. Layers are one of the keys to loving winter.

To make *every* season an invitation to stillness and snow-day-worthy coziness, add layers to your home by draping blankets over the arm of a chair or the back of a couch, where they are easy to grab. Invest in a pair of soft slippers and a comforting sweater to throw on in the evenings. Add an extra pillow to your reading nook, wear a lightweight scarf, or have a wide-brimmed hat ready for nature walks.

TRY THIS: HOT CHOCOLATE

There's a lot of comfort in holding a hot drink in your hands, taking slow sips, and letting in its warmth—even if you don't live in a cold climate. Enjoying a cup of tea, coffee, or hot chocolate aids relaxation and provides an emotional boost. It's like giving yourself a hug. Here's a favorite homemade hot chocolate recipe to add to your routine in those moments you want to take it easy:

¼ cup sugar   4 cups milk   ½ cup chocolate chips
¼ cup cocoa powder   ¾ tsp. vanilla

Whisk together equal parts sugar and cocoa powder in a saucepan, then add in the milk, vanilla, and chocolate chips. Whisk constantly over medium heat until it begins to steam. Pour into a favorite mug. Top with whipped cream, mini chocolate chips, peppermint chips, or marshmallows.

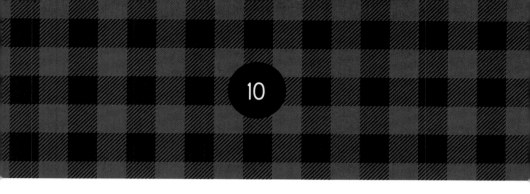

THE FOREST FOR
THE TREES

*And let us not grow weary of doing good, for in due
season we will reap, if we do not give up.*

GALATIANS 6:9 ESV

W e are well on our way. Now we just need to be focused and brave enough
to stay the course. How do we keep the momentum moving forward
when we feel like we have been working so hard, for so long, and our dream
still seems far away? How do we keep our focus and avoid getting sidetracked?
Are you on your way now, or are you feeling stuck?

It can be easy to get lost in all the details and lose sight of the big picture.
We need to be careful if we can't see the forest for the trees. This is when we
can step back and keep the vision, the big picture, of where we are heading
and why we want to go that way. It's important to maintain perspective and
navigate around what gets in our way.

Where I live, we are surrounded by forest. It's thick and beautiful. It draws
another analogy for me as I think about keeping the journey constantly growing

forward. Many of the obstacles to our dreams can feel like a forest of trees lining up to block our way. If we can get a handle on a few of the biggest trees rather than being hindered by the forest's density, we can make it through. Grace can replace guilt. We can set the right expectations and find a comfortable balance.

THE BIG PICTURE

One of my favorite settings on my phone's camera is panorama. Being able to take a photo of the entire scene in front of me is breathtaking. It leaves nothing out; I can take it all in. Then as I choose to, I can zoom in and focus on the details.

That's an important action when working toward our goals as well. We can refocus on which details need our time and attention each day and determine what can wait or what doesn't matter or belong in the journey anymore. I think about that as I look at my to-do lists. I have a calendar with a list to indicate when I want to have milestones checked off, but I also take time at the end of the week to set out my benchmarks for the week ahead. Then each afternoon or evening, I review these notes for the following day.

That calendar—the big-picture view of where I'm headed—is on my inspiration board. By breaking down the to-dos into manageable chunks over time, my goals don't overwhelm me.

COMFORT IN CAPACITY

My husband laughs every time we head out on a trip, even short ones, because I am stuffed into the front seat, happy as can be, surrounded by all my favorite things. It drives him a bit crazy. He doesn't understand how I can be comfortable with all that "stuff" around me. For me, it's a happy place, with my books, magazines, computer, and journal.

It makes me think about our personal internal capacities: what we can fit into our lives, into our days. The capacity comfort level will be different for each person. It's for us to notice what our capacity is when we embark on our

dream. We can't be everything or do all the things. To pursue our dreams in a healthy, sustainable way, we must recognize what we can fit in and then be comfortable sticking to limits and boundaries to protect our margins.

I've heard it said that if the devil can't make you naughty, he'll make you busy. We can fill our days with too much. Often, we may very well be adding great opportunities, meaningful moments, and goodness, but when we have a goal ahead of us, we must not get sidetracked by busyness. We need a clear vision of where we want to go, and we must consciously decide what doesn't fit. I struggle with this a lot.

There are priorities in my life that require protection and space so they remain part of the dream. Time with my family and friends. My faith, fitness, and pursuit of fun. But I won't be able to say yes to every social activity or church opportunity, even the ones that align with my priorities. Remember, your no doesn't require an explanation, excuse, or apology.

We owe it to our dreams and our daily lives to give ourselves the gift of time to decide, to evaluate if we have the space or desire to commit to something. Keep in mind that our capacity will be at different levels in different seasons of life.

> TO PURSUE OUR DREAMS IN A HEALTHY, SUSTAINABLE WAY, WE MUST RECOGNIZE WHAT WE CAN FIT IN AND THEN BE COMFORTABLE STICKING TO LIMITS AND BOUNDARIES TO PROTECT OUR MARGINS.

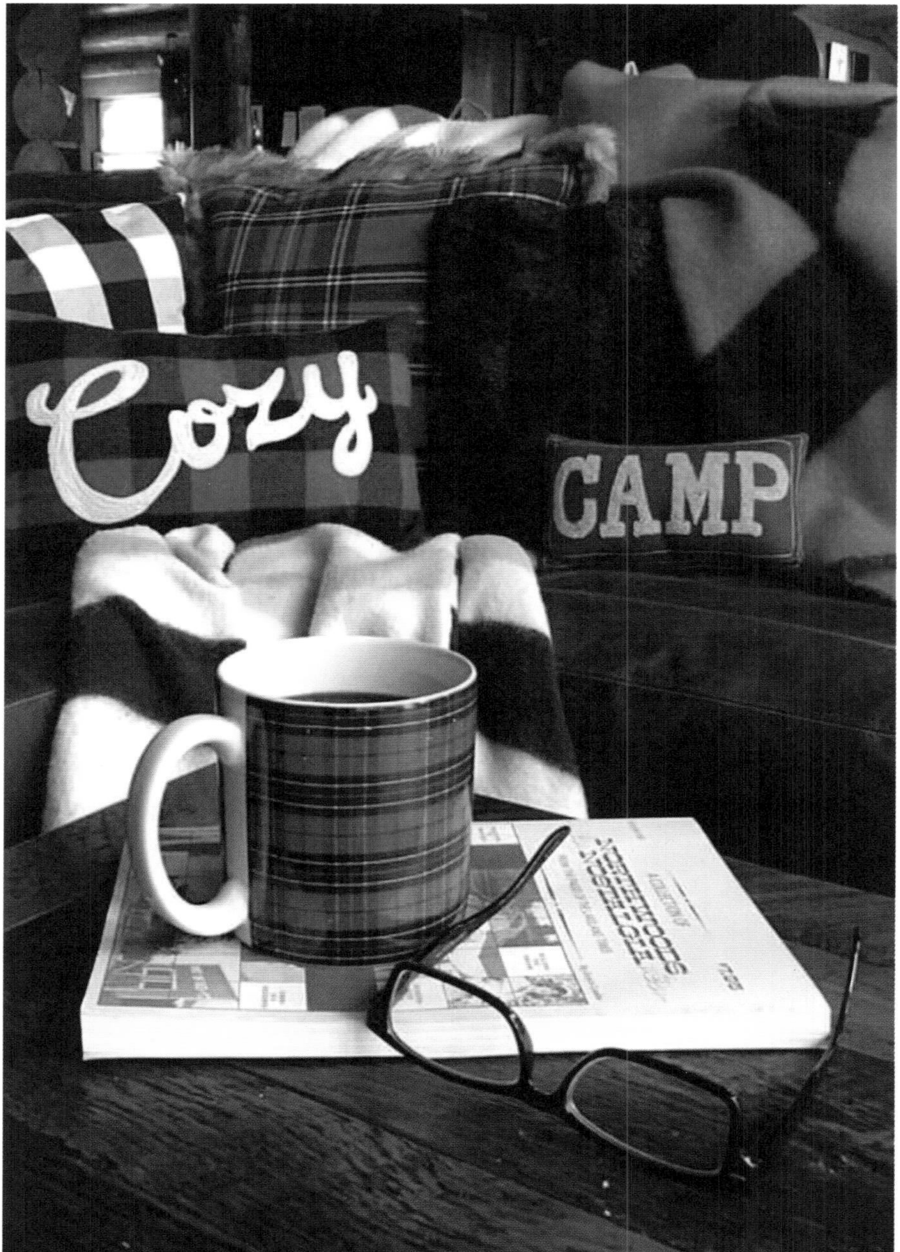
Cozy
CAMP

A DIFFERENT PATH

There may come a point when we become aware that what we have been spending time working toward is not going to be possible. Obstacles may come into view that we cannot get around and are beyond our control. It's important to realize that even though this brings a great deal of disappointment, we will have learned a lot and grown in big ways. When life then takes us down a different path, we may find joy there. Soon we'll understand how each previous step, decision, and preserved priority has guided us toward the new direction.

When my first child was born, I was teaching elementary school. I loved every minute of teaching and spending time with my coworkers, with the students, and at the school. But I had a dream to stay home as much as possible with my daughter. I decided to take a break from the classroom and start my own tutoring and enrichment business. A fellow teacher was excited to take the journey with me.

We rented a space in a strip mall near the school we had been teaching at and decorated it with a campy, woodsy theme. (This was about 15 years before I even knew the Northwoods existed and that someday I'd live in a lakeside log cabin!) Families signed up their kids for individual tutoring and for our small group workshops.

JOURNAL THE JOURNEY

- What struggles do you face when finding your correct capacity?

- What are you excited about at this point in your journey?

- Are you feeling a tug to change direction or step back from the dream you've been working toward? Write about your feelings to get more clarity.

In the back room, we set up an area where we could bring our little ones to be watched by a sitter. So during the daytime hours, we were home with our kids, and for a few after-school hours, we worked while our littles were still nearby.

It was such a fun journey, but after a year, we decided to go back into the classroom. Financially, it wasn't working. But I have not one single regret for trying! Creating something, from idea to reality, was an unbelievable experience. Yes, there were things we could have tweaked and adjusted, but there was much to be proud of. From where I am now, I can see how that time laid some building blocks for my future. I couldn't see it then, but God knew. When my friend and I decided to close, we did so knowing that God had wanted us to do our business for that time period only. He removed the desire from our hearts, and we were certain closing was the right decision.

Every time we try, every time we step toward a dream, every time we fall but get back up, we are building ourselves up inside.

One of my family's favorite activities at the cabin is to sit around the campfire out back. We have a big stack of wood waiting to be used to build fires. I like to think our attempts, our times of trying, and our lessons learned are like that stack of wood. Each piece is an experience. Each piece is a book we've read, a podcast we've listened to, encouragement from a friend or mentor. When we begin to dream a new dream, we can pull from that "woodpile," stack up the pieces we need, and light a fire. Our fire will burn consistently and ignite in us the passion we need to go and grow toward the goals we set.

EXPECTATION REVISIONS

Expectations can give us energy or drain us. The expectancy of what's to come may give us a boost. We may be encouraged to spend time visualizing ourselves already achieving our goals, holding the trophy. I do think that's a great practice. But we need to find the tipping point between believing in amazing possibilities and being realistic. Too-big expectations can leave us prone to

discouragement when plans go awry. On the flip side, being too stuck in reality can make us our own worst critics.

One of the things I must often do is revise my expectations. When my tutoring and enrichment business didn't continue, I had to revise my expectations and close that chapter with grace. Revising our expectations may come into play daily as we encounter detours and difficulties. This doesn't have to take us off the path. We can pause to evaluate and then move forward with renewed conviction and confidence in the direction we are going.

There may be times when you work toward a goal that turns out not to be one you will see through to the end. You may only be called to get something started. Maybe you take a leadership role in an organization to start a new initiative you have passion for. As you lead, it starts to make some progress, but when you leave office and your successor takes over, it really gains traction. Embrace the joy of playing an initiating role, and celebrate and cheer on those who take the dream the rest of the way.

REVISING OUR EXPECTATIONS MAY COME INTO PLAY DAILY AS WE ENCOUNTER DETOURS AND DIFFICULTIES. THIS DOESN'T HAVE TO TAKE US OFF THE PATH. WE CAN PAUSE TO EVALUATE AND THEN MOVE FORWARD WITH RENEWED CONVICTION AND CONFIDENCE IN THE DIRECTION WE ARE GOING.

FIND A WAY OUT OF THE WOODS

When we feel stuck, we can remember to stop, stand on our solid foundation, pull out the "resources" we've packed, consult God's arrows, and walk forward out of the woods supported and empowered by prayer, Scripture, fellowship, good habits, and healthy relationships.

Prayer: Before deciding or taking a next step, we should first talk to God—even before our spouse, mom, sister, or friends. He's the one who already knows how our story will go, so asking Him for guidance becomes the most insightful and natural part of our day.

Scripture: So many of our questions and concerns have already been addressed and answered in the Bible. Don't forget to search in your Bible or online to find the many verses relevant to the needs and hopes on your mind. I head to my Bible and highlight or underline relevant passages, putting a date next to them and thanking Him for the reminder.

Fellowship: I am amazed at how many times, in church or at Bible study, something that has been on my heart and mind is touched on in the lesson or through a verse or story. God uses our time in fellowship to provide encouragement and feed our spirits. These moments of feeling seen and known remind us we are not alone.

Good habits: It's essential to build our good habits—those we set for the mornings and others we incorporate into our days. Discern when to add new ones or replace bad ones. Adding one small adjustment at a time

or one new step in our routine can build up to big changes. It's commonly said that it takes 21 days to form a habit and 60 for it to become automatic. I find that if I try starting a new habit for just three days, I already begin to feel success.

Healthy relationships: It's natural to become like the people you surround yourself with. So prioritize time with those people you've identified who are positive, encouraging, and supportive. As they are also building flourishing lives, they will make great company for your pursuit of the same.

Whether we decide to keep going in the same direction, follow a new arrow, or stay content right where our feet are, if we are listening and watching for God's leading, we will end up in the right spot.

BLAZE A TRAIL
FORM A FOUNDATION OF SUCCESSES

Our lives flourish if we build on a foundation using the right materials. My cabin home serves as a great visual. Our place is a full log cabin built like a kid's toy in real life. Logs are strategically stacked together, and all the electrical, plumbing, and HVAC systems run through the inside of the logs. There is a plan for the enduring design. Each log serves the stability of the whole.

Grab a Jenga set, and pour all the pieces into a pretty bowl. You can set it on the corner of your desk. As you hit milestones along your journey, write a note on a block and include the date. Begin stacking your blocks as you write in your accomplishments. Even if it was something hard that you overcame, it's great to include the memory. As your tower grows, you will have a great visual of your success.

WISDOM ALONG THE WAY

That person is like a tree planted by streams of water,
which yields its fruit in season
and whose leaf does not wither—whatever they do prospers.

PSALM 1:3

He cut down cedars, or perhaps took a cypress or oak.
He let it grow among the trees of the forest, or
planted a pine, and the rain made it grow.

ISAIAH 44:14

So then, just as you received Christ Jesus as Lord, continue to live
your lives in him, rooted and built up in him, strengthened in the
faith as you were taught, and overflowing with thankfulness.

COLOSSIANS 2:6–7

NORTHWOODS CONNECTION

One of my favorite activities to enjoy in the Northwoods is spending time around the campfire. It's a great way to gather with friends and loved ones. Often, there's lots of storytelling going on. There's laughter, sharing, music, and fun. Sometimes the fireside can also be quiet and reflective. It can be the perfect spot to sit and think. Time around the fire can also spark deep conversation. It might be the perfect spot to share your dreams with those gathered around or get feedback from a friend. Sitting by the fire in the evenings can be a great time to gaze into the changing colors of the flames, contemplate your day, and plan for the next.

It's a beautiful time to also do a little stargazing, looking up and remembering God's goodness and power. Giving gratitude in moments like this or pouring out our hearts in praise can come easy, but finding yourself speechless may happen too. Savor the awe.

TRY THIS: S'MORES

S'mores are a must-have around the campfire. Everyone gets very particular about how toasty they like their marshmallows. If you are like me, you like them soft and golden. Others in my family love to catch them on fire, blow them out, and enjoy the crunchy crust. Then when it comes to how to sandwich the marshmallow, the possibilities are endless. Here are a few favorite ways to try:

SWEET + SALTY
marshmallow
chocolate covered pretzels
2 graham cracker halves

PEANUT BUTTER
CHOCOLATE
marshmallow
peanut butter cup
2 chocolate cookies

DOODLES
marshmallow
chocolate
2 snickerdoodles

BERRY SWEET
marshmallow
strawberry slices
Nutella
2 graham crackers halves

ADVENTURE AWAITS

Thanks for letting me be a small part of your journey. I hope you have found encouragement in the reminders of who you are: uniquely made with a purpose and dreams planted in your heart. God wants you to grow toward a life that thrives.

A peek into the special connections my life in the Northwoods provides gives me insight into the lessons God's taught me over the last few years as I've chased my dreams. I hope my story and perspective hearten you for yours. It's been an honor to share and travel with you.

One of the most thrilling parts of the dream journey is that it never ends. We never fully "get there." We continue growing, learning, adjusting, and setting new dreams over the years. We must fall in love with the process and the chance to experience it all.

Keep journaling as you go. Start a new journal every year or with each change of direction. It will help you keep processing and be a wonderful reminder of how far you've come. Keep using your map (God's Word) as you travel closer and closer to True North (God) and the flourishing life He has planned for you. Don't give up. You may just change the world, your neighborhood, your family, or—last but not least—your journey through this life.

Keep your perspective beyond today, and pay attention to the divine guidance coming your way—the arrows pointing you forward. Pay attention to those dreams you have in your heart, and follow the arrows.

What you do will matter.

Life has changed a lot recently, and you will find your way.

You have the courage to try.

You have what it takes to make what you're doing great.

You can gather the gumption to go in a new direction.

You are enough.

PROJECT LIST

ACKNOWLEDGMENTS

Acknowledgments are actually one of my favorite parts of a book to read. It's the reminder that we are not on the adventure alone, and I surely have not been solo on mine.

A big thank you goes out to my agent, Teresa Everson of the William K. Jensen Literary Agency, for your limitless patience, encouragement, and guidance as my story went from a conversation to a published book. It was a big journey and a dream come true. You were the greatest guide and a true gift!

To KariAnne Wood: I'll never forget sitting in your dining room during the Inspire Conference when after hearing my story and dreams you told me "I should buckle up for the ride" and connected me to Teresa. Thank you for all the encouragement, your open heart to share, and "amazing" support!

To Ruth Samsel: I'm so grateful and blessed for the wisdom I glean every time we talk. Thanks for being an amazing inspiration and always cheering me on.

Thanks to Hope Lyda: With you, my words came to life. With you, words become art.

To the rest of the amazing team at Harvest House: I always encourage being surrounded by positive, uplifting people. You are exactly that to me.

To Diana and my team at White Arrows Home: What a joy that I get to work with you. Diana, two words: taffy shop.

To friends from every path I've traveled and turn I've taken: You have filled my memory box and made the journey so fun.

Most especially to my husband, Brian: Thank you for always supporting my ideas and trusting me to try. Each adventure is all the more amazing because you are with me.

To my kids, Kallin, Barron, Landry, Brooks, and Nazar: I learn the most about being brave and faithful from you. I am so lucky to be your mom. It is my greatest joy.

ABOUT THE AUTHOR

Kristin Lenz is a writer, a podcaster, and the creator of the popular blog and lifestyle brand White Arrows Home. She has a passion for encouraging women and helping them find greater connection and direction in their lives. Kristin and her husband live in the beautiful Northwoods of Wisconsin. They have five children, a Great Pyrenees dog, and two Bernese mountain dogs.